SOUL SEARCHING:
A Handbook for Discovering, Developing, and Talking about Your Spirituality

D1310692

NATHAN R. KOLLAR

ISBN: 1479145521
ISBN-13: 9781479145522
Library of Congress Control Number: 2012916149
CreateSpace Independent Publishing Platform
North Charleston, South Carolina

DEDICATION

To Rudolph, Eleanor, Rudy, and Judy; to David, Carrie, Laura, Camille, Sharon, Todd, and Jean who share the spiritual journey with me. May your voices always bring joy, your tears the necessary water for love's growth, and your touch the warmth for needed compassion. You have helped me discover the promises of the future and urged me to fulfill them. Thank you!

ACKNOWLEDGEMENTS

This book has taken a lifetime to experience and research. It never would have been finished without the expertise and encouragement of Carol, Libby, Bonnie, Bill, and Mohammad—and, of course, Jean, whose love surrounded every thought and struggle I experienced to get the words just right.

An everlasting thanks to all those who participated in the retreats, seminars, classes of theology or religious studies, workshops, and hours of spiritual direction – your spirit enlivens everything that follows.

TABLE OF CONTENTS

INTRODUCTION

Day 1, hour 1, minute 1, second 1.

The contestant opened the door and walked into the large well decorated living room. A tall, elderly, grey-haired man calmly limped toward him.

But the room! The room was filled with vibrant colored hands. From floor to ceiling each wall was covered with framed photos, paintings, sketches, and carvings of hands. On shelves, tables, and end tables were carved wooden and marble hands.

As the contestant sought to comprehend what enveloped him, the old man suddenly stood before him with hand outstretched and whispered "Hello. I am so happy to meet you. I spent over a year trying to find you. I hope you can help me."

"Me?" the contestant said. "What can I possibly do?"

"I need to know why this room has so many hands and who they belong to," said the man. "I looked for someone who possessed great attention to detail, sensitivity to people, and a critical mind accustomed to investigating complex mysteries. You easily won out over all the others."

Day 39, hour 2, minute 3, second 5

Since that first vote of confidence, the contestant worked tirelessly to answer the old man's questions. In the process, he learned that the man had been in a coma for ten years. When he woke, the official in charge of the long term care facility told him he had been in a plane crash ten years earlier. He was the lone survivor of what looked like a family of five. The charred remains of a deed for this house and a bank account of over one billion dollars were all that survived. Every attempt to discover his identity had failed. The old man was seventy-five, in reasonably good health, but was filled with anxiety over what had happened and why all evidence of his past was hidden. He felt this room of hands was the answer to his questions.

The contestant, whose name was Jack, had carefully examined the hands. That's why he arranged for this second meeting with the old man. Jack discovered that there were hands representing every age: from infancy to old age. After arranging the hands according to age he then began to notice that some had common marks on them such as scars, calluses, and bruises and some did not have any marks. But the marks were not random. Instead they were cumulative: if several had only calluses then several more had calluses and scars. Finally the oldest ones had all the marks: calluses, scars,, and wrinkled skin.

Jack rose from the stuffed chair as the man shuffled toward him. Jack shook the old man's hand and exchanged small talk. As he did so, he led the man toward a long table in the center of the room and began to explain his way of arranging the hands. The table was long and wide; covered with photos of the hands in the room. The youngest hands on the left gradually progressed to the older ones on the right. As the man slowly looked at what Jack had done, he rearranged the hands accord-

ing to the categories: the bruises, the bruises and the scar, the scar, the scar and calluses, the scarred old hands. He looked at the final arrangement of the photos; lifted his left hand and placed it over the last photo he had arranged; took several steps back from the table and tilted his head looking at the surrounding walls; first to the right, then the center and finally the left side of the room.

"It's me," he said.

"They are me."

Day 365, Hour 8, Minutes 6, Second 6

Jack had left the house two months ago. He was able to help identify the hands but not answer the question as to —why they were there. The old man began calling himself "Anton," after St. Anthony, the saint of lost causes. Every time Anton walked into the room of hands he learned something new. The scars on his left hand, for example, were matched by similar ones on his left leg. The calluses on the hands were of two types: those on the younger hands suggested they were from carpentering; those on the middle aged ones from playing a great deal of golf. So many hands. So many marks. So many more questions to ask and find answers to. So few years left to find the answers. What to do?

Anton was sitting on the rocker on the porch when he spied the young couple coming up the driveway. After a year of searching and several interviews he had invited them to come to live at the house for as long as they liked. He asked in return only that they help make the house a home for him and their family by improving on whatever they saw in need of improvement.

"Welcome. I'm so happy you accepted my offer. I hope you and your family find the place comfortable." With those words he led them into the house and its room of hands. Carefully he took a picture of their infant son's hand; and theirs too. He looked forward to placing them somewhere in the room: to beginning life anew.

****

Many of us are like Anton. At some moment we awake to the infinite futures that lie before us but only have bits and pieces of our past and present to help chose the best future. Anton had his room of hands, home, and money. We have pictures, memories, family, co-workers, and friends. Our body, like his, has its scars, aches, and pains to hint at what happened in our past. What both Anton and we have in common are the desire to seek a future better than the present and the conviction that this desire can be satisfied. What we must find is a clear path, and a means to walk it. If we discover the path to satisfy our desire, we must expect change. This book helps you discover the path and understand the change. The hands, of course, are metaphors for the soul.

Your soul is like Anton's hands. It is marked by all the joys and sorrows of your past. It is marked by boredom and exultation; success and failures; deep friendships and spurned relationships. You may be aware of some of those marks, just as you may be conscious of some of your past. But seldom do you have the chance to see as many marks as possible; to understand the patterns that show who you are. This book enables you to do that: to search for your soul. Your soul is the unique "you." It is the response to a deep thirst for transcendence, change, that only you can bring about to yourself and to others. This thirst for transcendence results in habits that satiate that thirst. Just as Anton's hands reflect what he had done with his life, so your habits reflect what you have done with your life in response to this deep thirst for transcendence: to become more than you are right now.

Change and Spirituality

Change is part of every human life. The hands in Anton's room, our body, our mind, and our emotions — they all proclaim the change that surrounds us and the change that we are. To desire a future better than our present and past is to desire change. You might not think of it this way, but such a desire is also a desire for a spirituality.

Every spiritual life promises and promotes a vision and means to transform your present life into a better one. Each spiritual life promises and promotes the discovery of a wonderful soul. Your life will change whether you want it to or not. You cannot prevent your body from changing, your mind from being curious and thinking, nor your emotions from responding to daily events. In the face of continual change your choice is either to let it happen or control its happening: your body will change; exercise shapes that change; your mind will be curious and think; education directs the curiosity and provides methods for thinking to produce the best results; your emotions stimulate your interaction with your environment; parenting directs these emotions along constructive paths. Your soul is changing in response to your life changes. A spirituality helps direct that change. Your clock keeps ticking just as Anton's did.

Your choice is between a lazy spiritual life and a mature spiritual life. A lazy spiritual life lets change happen to you. A mature spiritual life accepts responsibility for the change that makes you who you are. This workbook is written to help you take responsibility for your spiritual growth. It provides you with a process for discovering your past and present spirituality; for searching among diverse spiritualities for what is necessary to develop a future spirituality; and, ways of choosing and evaluating what you have chosen to be your spiritual path.

The process consists of five chapters which will provide you with the information necessary to seek, find, and deepen your spirituality and five sets of interrogations, titled *Dear Diary*, which will stimulate your memory, mind, and feelings to nourish your spiritual quest. Although the chapters are placed before the Dear Diary questions I have found some readers prefer to do the Dear Diary before reading the content-oriented chapters. It's your choice.

What I have done here is condense the thoughts and experiences of the thousands of people I have engaged in spiritual discussions over the last five decades of my life. The discussions were in classes, workshops, retreats, and individually. What we learned is that a spiritual life grows only if we share it with others and compare it with one or more of the classic spiritualities. I have expanded the comparison to include spiritualities that, in the past, were on the margins of society. Today, some people have found solace in these marginal spiritualities. Only time will tell whether they have made a healthy choice, But since such spiritualities are present in our society, I thought it best to at least mention them.

I have also written another book as a companion to this one. *Spiritualities: Past, Present, and Future – An Introduction.* It offers an in-depth examination of the ideas and spiritualities presented here. If you find yourself asking why I am saying something, the answer to your question is found in *Spiritualities: Past, Present, and Future.* The footnotes in this book are few because all of the references are in the other one. Sometimes I have copied entire sections from the other book and placed them in this one. My emphasis here is to get you thinking and working on your spirituality. My emphasis in *Spiritualities* is to provide you with the thoughts of others and a more detailed description of the spiritualities that have flourished on this earth. Here we take the definition of spirituality I developed in *Spiritualities* and guide you in discovering your own. *A spirituality is a way of life that promises and promotes total transformative change in your life.* The rest of this workbook deals with your present way of life, what you see as your possible futures of that way of life, bringing that way of life into conversations with others, and then choosing the future you think best.

One last point before beginning: I will use the terms "wholistic" or "wholism" throughout the book. Many times dictionaries provide only one spelling for this word: holism. There are two reasons I retain the *w*. One is that we are whole. To sustain our wholeness we must pay equal attention to every part of our being: body, mind, soul, and spirit. To reduce us to only one of these manifestations of who we are deprives us of our humanity. The second reason is that the *w* in wholistic is like our arms stretching out to every living and nonliving being. We seek to touch, hear, see, taste, and smell. We are curious and thus we seek to know, understand, and connect with "the other" and "others." We are all this and more. We are whole. With our arms outstretched wide and our palms open, we seek to engage in the dance of life with everything and everyone. That is what it is all about—we must grow in our understanding of others so that we can grow in our spirituality and assist others in their spiritual growth.

Let us begin.

Chapter One

Building Spiritual Bridges

London Bridge is falling down, falling down,
My fair lady

Webster's dictionary provides over fifteen meanings for the
word spirit and the Encarta Thesaurus provides over
seventy words or phrases to take its place. A Google search
finds 41,800,000 sites for the word spirituality.

***

Your words are bridges to other cultures and other people. They link your past, present, and future. When they are uncertain, feeble structures, your way of life is threatened and, in turn, becomes uncertain and feeble. The bridges fall down.

In contemporary culture, the meaning of words easily shift when powerful groups want them to change for commercial, political, ideological, artistic, or personal reasons. Contemporary meanings of the word *spirituality* and *spiritual* reflect all these reasons for change. "Dear Diary I" will help you discern the meanings you have for spiritual and spirituality.

In this chapter, I will answer three questions: What are we talking about? How do we talk about it? How do we write and enter into conversation about it? The answers to these questions will enable you to have a clear idea of how the bridges around you are built before you approach them as avenues for building a spiritual life. Chapter Two will examine the essential structure of a spiritual life.

Are You Spiritual?

What are you talking about when you ask questions about *spiritual* and *spirituality*? We cannot take for granted that we know what those two words and their cognates mean because their meanings as found in dictionaries, websites, and conversation are increasing. A short history lesson provides us with the trends inherent in the increase.

A Foundational Experience: Breath, Life, Soul, Energy, and Spirit

Breathing and everything associated with it is foundational to human experience. Until recently, if you could not breathe on your own, you died. Breath in all its variations is a good indicator of life and all its diversity. How you breathe determines how well you sing, run, walk, sleep, and interact with others. Good breath equals good life; no breath equals death.

The Western tradition expresses this primary experience in its foundational story of human creation. In that story, God is described as breathing into the first human's nostrils—thus giving that person, and all subsequent humans, life (Genesis 2:7). When a person has good breath, he or she has energy, vitality, and life. The Greeks used the word *pneuma*, the Jews used *ruach*, the Hindus used *prana*. The words, and their associates, all refer to that primary experience of human living—breathing. These words also are translated into English as *spirit, soul, ghost,* and *energizing force*.

Whether our breath/spirit/soul/ghost/energizing force is immortal, separate from our identity, or totally one with the fleshy aspects of who we are, is a continual and essential aspect of philosophical and theological discussions. For the purposes of our present discussion, I offer the experience and the words that communicate this experience as a beginning point for the historical discussion of spirituality.

Spiritual People and Spiritual Communities

From its beginning, Christian tradition affirmed its Jewish roots by calling God Spirit and many times described God as the Holy Spirit. In the Christian tradition, which was the foundation of Western culture for over two thousand years, God was understood to be Father, Son, and Holy Spirit. Christians came to believe that God was not only incarnate in Jesus but also God, as the Holy Spirit, was part of every Christian's life. God breathed God's Holy Spirit into every Christian to enable him or her to live with God's life.

Each Christian was understood to be living the life of the Holy Spirit as a result of God's free gift (grace) to that Christian. Thus each Christian was understood to be living a spirit or spiritual life as a result of God's grace or free gift. A Christian's daily life was his or her spiritual life. This simple Christian reality produced libraries of books dealing with attempts to understand the nature of this gift, how to deepen its vitality in our life, and how to share it with others. It has also given birth to communities of people who dedicate their entire lives to stimulating the growth of God's life (Spirit) in their individual and communal lives.

The history of these men and women goes back to the very origins of Christianity. Their view of Christianity was influenced by a strong cultural view in Egypt and Greece that accepted as fact that one's soul was separate from the body and destined to live independent of the body forever. This trend toward emphasizing the soul or spirit as one's human essence over and against the body as mere heavy baggage preventing it from going to the heavens became part of the way Christians thought about living the life of the Holy Spirit—their spiritual life.

Spiritual life became more than living a good Christian life. It became a life dedicated to an increased sensitivity to God's presence by controlling one's body to perfect the life of the soul. Thus men and women who were serious about living that life did everything they could to train their bodies. Their way of leading a spiritual life always had a physical asceticism associated with it. Part of that asceticism began to be formulated into the vows of poverty (you should own nothing), chastity (you should not engage in sexual intercourse), and obedience (you should follow the will of those appointed by God).

Over the centuries charismatic leaders founded communities established around ideals and asceticisms unique to each of them. They gave birth to a diversity of ways of leading a spiritual life. Many of these communities still exist today—each with a unique spirituality evidenced in the way they live, the theologies that explain their spiritual life, the spiritual directors attuned to its implementation, and centuries of writings reflecting on their benefits for their follower.

By 1500 CE, this separation of body and spirit, along with the separation of those leading an intense spiritual life from everyone else, resulted in a way of speaking about spirituality that still exists among some Christians. Spirituality (*spiritualitas* in Latin) had two meanings: a mode of being and a way of acting. As a mode of being, it was the opposite of corporality in much writing. Legal writings, for example, reflected a division of life into the spiritual realm and the temporal realm. This latter legal application of *spiritualitas* easily gave way to talking about the spiritual in reference to the clergy and the temporal in reference to the laity.

The second interpretation narrowed the meaning of the spiritual realm to refer to those who lead the contemplative (spiritual) life. Such a life was one more closely aligned with the life of the mind, the mystical life, the devotional life. The "active" life in this sense was one that took one away from being spiritual. It was one of work, family, sensuality, and the ordinary. Leading a spiritual life meant that one was separate from those who did not lead it. It meant a strict discipline of one's body in every way possible to enhance the person's mental, contemplative, and spiritual existence. These distinctions between active and contemplative were challenged in subsequent centuries while the spiritualities that embodied them continued on.

New Meanings to Old Words Reflect New Spiritual Bridges Coming into Existence

From about 899 CE to 1450 CE, the word *religion* referred to those communities dedicated to leading a perfect spiritual life, which we just described. They were called religious communities. After the sixteenth century, the meaning of *religion* began to shift in Western culture to what we have today. The meaning of *spirituality* also changed to what we have today. Many in the West use the words *religion*, *spirituality*, and *society* presupposing that they mean something different.

Yet most people in the world speak and act as if they were one. What we call religious holidays are national holidays. What we accept as religious morality is proclaimed as the law of the land. What we teach as history is described as God's will. What we describe as the separation of church and state is seen as one community. The experiment of separating religion and state found in US law and professional literature affects our language and expectations. Certainly the acceptance or non-acceptance of such language will determine your spiritual life. You may, for example, be part of the large number of people who believe Christian prayer should be allowed in all public institutions and government funds should be used in the defense of Christianity at home and abroad.

Once people begin to separate religion and culture linguistically, the natural consequence is to ask, "What does religion mean?" By the end of the nineteenth century, scholars in the newly founded academic discipline of comparative religion offered answers that still influence many people writing about religion and spirituality. *Religion, they said, was an experience that we use to describe the sacred, mysterious, holy, or supernatural.*

People encountering a religious reality, they said, felt both attracted to and repelled by it at the same time. It was an awesome feeling. It was a mystic's experience of being swept up into the being of God; it was the enlightenment described by Siddhartha; it was the cry of Muhammad in response to the angel shaking him and commanding him to recite. It was also the feeling you might have in realizing that someone loves you; the feeling you might have when alone skiing down a mountain or running a marathon and getting into the "zone." If you have ever had the experience or feeling that you are in the presence of something overwhelmingly powerful, wishing you could stay there and yet frightened out of your wits at what would happen if you did, then you have had an intense sacred experience. Religions were understood to provided the principal sources of that sacred experience.

Previous to when scholars were comparing world religions, there were a series of movements in the United States called Great Awakenings and revivals. Most preachers of revival emphasized emotion and feelings rather than church law and doctrine. They said that the feeling of being saved, of the Spirit's movement, and of the certainty of the Bible were central to one's relationship with God. Following the norms of religious institutions was not life giving because one could not feel any spiritual life in institutions.

The sacred experience of the scholars and the born-again experience of the preachers dominated American culture's view of religion and spirituality. They seldom attended to other experiences that were also constitutive of religion and spirituality. These too were deeply felt and associated with leading a religious and spiritual life.

A common spiritual feeling that is seldom mentioned is *duty and obedience* to a cause, a community, or a person. People are called followers and disciples as a consequence of this experience. Many times they are willing to sacrifice their life and fortune at the behest of their lord, master, king, general, or leader. *Justice*, as an experience and as a desired lifestyle for everyone, causes people and communities to sacrifice all for the experience of living with others who seek fairness in society and within oneself.

Some spiritualities conceptualize the life after death as one that satisfies this need for justice, honesty, and integrity. Belief in heaven, hell, and karma are examples of this same experiential expectation. *Discipline*, as a consistent way of life, is seen by most spiritualities as necessary to leading any kind of spirituality. What use is it if we say one thing and do something else; do something one day and its opposite the next? *Consistency* is essential to a spiritual life. So too is *hope*. *Optimism* is seen as the mark of a spiritual person because he or she expects life to be better than it is right now. Finally, many spiritualities are based on the conviction that there is *a power or energy independent of everything and everyone we experience*. This is expressed in stories of the creation of the world, daily miracles, and power to destroy the world. This is found, too, in a deep fear some people have that a god will cause them suffering here or in the hereafter. These experiences and convictions may be found in most spiritualities, even though they are usually not attended to in as much detail as experiences of the sacred, the holy, and the supernatural by writers and researchers.

The beginning of the twenty-first century saw books such as the following at the top of the best- seller lists and promoted as spiritual literature: *Eat, Pray, Love: One Woman's Search for Everything Across Italy, India and Indonesia*, by Elizabeth Gilbert;[1] *A Course in Weight Loss: 21 Spiritual Lessons for Surrendering Your Weight Forever* by Marianne Williamson;[2] *The 5 Love Languages: The Secret to Love That Lasts* by Gary Chapman;[3] *The Power of Now: A Guide to Spiritual Enlightenment* by Eckhart Tolle;[4] *Be Love Now: The Path of the Hear,* by Ram Dass and Rameshwar Das.[5] These books reflect the broadening of the definition of spirituality to include methods of self-help and the goal of individual betterment.

This broadening of our understanding of *spirituality* results in the inclusion of marginal spiritualities such as Wicca and the title of *spirituality* becoming dependent on experience rather than lifestyle. Whatever and whoever provides you with an experience of transcendence that takes you away from the ordinary, everyday life you live is now considered spiritual. *The trend is toward a transcendent experience as the norm for being titled a spirituality.* The connection to a set of signposts that build a sustainable set of habits to enable the creation of a new life and a new society is loosened. In the place of this connection is the immediate satiation of one's transcendent desire and a search for a lifestyle that will continually fill this desire.

The twenty-first century in the United States also reflected the interplay between American religion, religious pluralism, the burgeoning self-help movements, and the distrust of traditional religious authorities. As a consequence, many of those seeking a spiritual life reflect this interplay resulting in the following characteristics of many American spiritualities:

- *Witness.* A person's spirituality should result in an authentic enthusiasm ready to be shared with all. He or she should be conscious that he or she is spiritual and have the ready words and physical countenance to disseminate it.
- *Quick life change.* A good spirituality should produce results within a few weeks or months in the devotee's life.
- *Personal betterment.* "I" must benefit physically, socially, and psychologically from living a spiritual life.
- *Distrust of institutions.* Spontaneity and informality best express the vitality of a spiritual world.
- *Conscious promotion of spiritual basics.* Spiritual basics provide the means of entering into, coping with, and coming out of those transformative events that challenge all of us: birth, suffering, marriage, death, job, personal relationships, and self-image. An important part of such provision is providing repetitive procedures for achieving these results. Examples of repetitive procedures are ways of breathing, thinking (for example, positive thoughts, meditation), wearing clothes, such as a ribbon wrapped around one's wrist, and following the twelve steps or ten commands..
- *New revelations.* The revelation provides the devotee with a feeling of starting life anew and discovering something that the

majority of people are unaware of. The "new" may be in the unearthing of ancient books, ideas, ways of life, or methods of spirituality. The "new" may be experienced in the appearance of an angel, spirit, or other worldly vision.

- *Expert spiritual guides* are found through the Internet, print literature (books and magazines), and word of mouth. These are "expert" because they are important witnesses to a spiritual experience. Some guides claim previous, other-worldly existence. Many guides witness to traveling the world in search of spiritual insight and, once having found it, dedicating their lives to sharing it with others.

- *Shopping for a spirituality* contains two important contemporary American values: choice and freedom. The freedom to choose and the choice itself demonstrate the spirituality's vitality—that is, if a lot of people are choosing it, it must be good. Style and fads in spirituality are as important as those in the rest of life.

A Transcendent Goal and Means of Transformation Should be Part of Every Spirituality

Hopefully, what we have reviewed has touched on your way of answering the question "Are You Spiritual?" There is, I would suggest, an underlying experience on which all of these descriptions of spirituality are based and one which you have had. This is the experience of going beyond your immediate sense of self, place, and time—the experience of transcendence. Transcendence is sensual even while it may originate in our minds, wills, and emotions. It is the impulse that enlivens every moment of our life. It is the desire for "more" of life than what we have right now and the need to find the means to satisfy the need for more. The desire for transcendence, for more, is always present within each of us seeking to move beyond the here and now to another reality. We see such desire in a small child spinning in a circle to experience a world beyond the ordinary and a person drinking or doing drugs to experience something different. We have thousands upon thousands of ways of entering into these other modes of existence: art, stories, music, work, play, and religion, to name a few. Seeking transcendence is part of being human. Seeking and living transcendence is also the essential ingredient of a spiritual life. If we are fortunate, we may briefly enter into this other world of alternate reality promised by a spiritual life. Certainly each *spiritual life promises and promotes the vision and means to change the present into this other, better, future world in the near or distant future.* To live a spiritual life, we must be aware of what is promised and the means that bring us into its alternate reality.

This is a very difficult task, since we can never be completely sure of what that new world is or will be. When we deal with the completion of a spiritual way of life, we are describing an ultimate transcendence: a world totally different from the one we live in at this moment in time and space. Words in common usage such as *heaven, hell, nirvana,* and *enlightenment* give us the impression that we know what ultimate transcendence is. Actually, all these are bumbling attempts in word and stories fail to give us a sense of what this totally other existence is like.

How Do You Talk about Your Spiritual Life?

Learning to Talk

Our words and their intended meanings are part of who we are. Nature and nurture are always part of trying to understand the spiritual self. Certainly both nature and nurture contribute to our expression of who we are and who we wish to be. We make our choices because of both our genetic makeup and the people who influence us throughout our lives. These choices are embedded in thoughts, ideas, ideals, words, and actions.

Socialization is the process by which the people we live with influence how we think and act. It embeds language distinctions, such as body, soul, spirit, and mind, as well as languages that make no such distinctions;

moral understandings, such as karma or divine judgment; and life goals such as the kingdom of God and nirvana. It even determines time sensitivity, such as feeling our life is going somewhere or our life is an illusion best let happen because we can't do anything about it.

How we talk about our spiritual life and our expectations about our spiritual life are dependent on our socialization process. A typical example of socialization in Western cultures is identifying spirituality with God. Such identification would lead us to seek God's role in our life and to become more aware of God's role in it by seeking to deepen our spirituality. Contrarily, a rejection of God would be seen as a rejection of all desire for a spiritual life, or involvement with God may be seen as destructive of a proper maturation process.

In this instance, socialization provides the dominant structure for spiritual discussions and expectations. This workbook is designed to make you aware of spiritualities beyond your immediate expectations. It is helpful, therefore, to have some idea of what that process is. An understanding of socialization also enables you to have some idea of what has to occur when you begin to encounter ideas and practices that are not part of your socialization process.

Here is an example using the Roman Catholic practice of genuflecting before the sacred bread, or host, which is believed to be a way Jesus is present to us. First we learn how to act (kneel in church). Then we recognize the feeling associated with such an action (reverence). Then the norms associated with such actions and feelings (only in church, in a certain direction), and the ideas associated with such actions, feelings, and norms develop (Jesus is present in the bread up in the front of the church, so kneel and feel reverent). Finally, we question the behavior, feelings, norms, and ideas in order to modify them into a better way than at present. (In Asia, for example, we bow to show reverence; it's perceived as better than the medieval habit of kneeling; and rice bread is better than wheat bread for the Lord's Supper.)

This socialization process usually goes unnoticed as we grow up. And most people never arrive at the last stage.[6] This growing up is a process of both our entering more deeply into the life of the community and the community's increased recognition of us as an authentic member of that community. The entire process is happening subconsciously in a complex and systemic manner.

Talking and Listening

At their best, the spiritual words we have been socialized into speaking place us at that still moment and place of transformation that offers us a choice for more life. The "*om*" (aum) chanted by the Buddhist monk and the declaration "*Et verbum caro factum est*" (the word made flesh) by a traditionalist Catholic bishop are ancient words resounding throughout the culture and across the world, declaring the here and now of spiritual revolution. For those of the Eastern religious heritage the word *om* chanted or written is the means of transcending to a new life. For those of the Christian tradition, joining oneself to the thought and action of the Word made flesh (Jesus) is the height of mystical experience and the means of building God's kingdom on earth.

Words are fragile symbols presenting infinite, eternal possibilities. Any tangible means of transformation may be a spiritual word. Spiritual words are filled with the promise of all the experiences associated with the sacred. They are symbols that promise and promote our spiritual life. As symbols, they can be encountered with all the senses. They are felt more than thought about, even as the experience leads into new and deeper thoughts.

When words are part of a cultural language, they are classics: always growing while deeply rooted in the past. They connect our past, present, and future. As symbols, words may be experienced in many ways and at various levels. The *om* chanted by an experienced monk may lead to a mystical experience one day and a yawn the next. The declaration of Jesus as savior may lead one person to a newly engaged way of life and another to a narrow, dogmatic isolationism.

A symbol has many meanings. When reduced to one, it becomes a sign and loses its ability to gather a large number of people onto a spiritual path—excluding those who embrace another meaning for the symbol. As you begin your spiritual journey, words of all types will enable you to enter into conversation with your life through your diary and with the diverse spiritualities presented in this book. This conversation is an opportunity for spiritual growth.

Spiritual Listening

A spirituality is *a way of life seeking a beneficial transformation and transcendence of self and community.* Spiritual listening is striving to hear the whole while attending to one symbol within the whole such as words, gestures, touch, smell, or relationships. In "hearing" that symbol, one engages his or her entire way of life. Perhaps the easiest image here is the common visual image in children's movies where a mirror is used to enter into another world. The child goes to the mirror, touches it, and walks through it into another world, a world not sensed before going into the mirror. A spiritual symbol is similar to that mirror. Under the proper conditions, we enter into a spiritual way of life by encountering the symbols through listening—a way of life that portrays and offers the means to transform this present world in and through its words, actions, and communal life.

This way of life provides direction and purpose to individual and communal living. Feasts and fasts direct our calendar and our eating. Moral imperatives direct our sexual life, commerce, war, and conversations. Thus, for example, we "listen" to an individual who silently kneels, bows, and raises his or her hands to the heavens three times a day. Our listening initially reveals the gestures and the time. Further listening opens our minds to his or her view of the universe. Its cause, and our relation to that cause, changes everything. In the depths of this listening, we open ourselves to the mysterious, awe-filled transcendence that connects each being to each other.

In our spiritual lives, we deal with patterns and symbols. In spiritual listening, we have the opportunity through people's words and actions to become part of the larger reality they symbolize—a larger reality we can encounter only through the particular pattern of symbols that constitute a spiritual life. And the encounter with a symbol means we are caught up in a world of many meanings, feelings, and relationships.

The foundational rubric of spiritual listening is to *listen to the whole person, not only his or her spirituality and/or religion.* Spirituality alone does not exist. Spiritual people do. This spiritual dimension of their person-hood will become evident as we focus on them in their entirety. Listen to their story, and seek to understand their pattern. Listen to their words, their actions, their meanings, and their feelings, not isolated one from another but whole—connected to each other. In the listening, we become aware of the spirituality who they are. In hearing their pattern, their tune, we become part of the spiritual symphony of the universe. As a symbol of a spiritual way of life, they enable us to enter that aspect of our world that is hopeful, changing, and striving to better everything and everyone around them and their community. From this perspective, *true spiritual listening is listening to individual and communal yearnings to change the self and the world for the better as evidenced in their words as expressive of their way of life.*

Respectful Listening: A Means of Entering into a Spiritual Conversation

Respectful listening is key to a spiritual conversation with one's self and with others. We must honor our past, present, and future as well as those of others. It seems that the most publicized method of talking and listening in our culture is adversarial—we listen only to demean the other, catch the other up in word games, and paint an image of the other that is repulsive to the audience. That is why many pundits and politicians speak in loud, short sentences for brief periods, repeating the same message over and over. Respectful listening by everyone in the conversation honors the words, ideas, and feelings of the speaker and the listener. Respectful listening begins by honoring the speaker as valuable and unique both to himself or herself and to us.

When you sense you know how the other person feels and are able to accurately repeat the ideas of what the other person says, you know that you are listening. When you can "read" the individual's body language and find value in who the person is, you know you are listening to him or her. When you are not interrupting, giving advice, jumping to conclusions, arguing, or letting the person's words or feelings stimulate yours too quickly, you know you are listening. Listening is a learned skill. It must be practiced. With practice you gradually realize you do not need to defend yourself constantly, and that receptive silence does not indicate you have anything to say. Respectful listening is a skill that demands continual practice with children, coworkers, friends, and the significant people in your life to do well.

When a conversation is going well, we never think of words, of meaning, of how people gesture, of their spirituality, of their facial features, or even of who they are. When things are going well, we enter into a zone of collegiality and understanding that may produce laughter, sorrow, joy, and even hate, since collegiality may have many forms and purposes—good as well as evil. When it is not going well, we find ourselves oozing negative attitudes toward the speaker, such as anger, hate, and destructive competitiveness. We find ourselves not hearing what is being said but what we expect to hear. We find ourselves dismissing the speaker as perhaps a fool, an ignorant lout, or provocateur. In any case, the speaker is "opposed" to us.

How do we practice collegial spiritual listening when we do not like the person and find him or her offensive in every way? We can listen only if we have reasons to listen and hopes of building a positive attitude toward the person.

This optimism is based on our conviction that we have the necessary listening skills and that the person we are listening to is as valuable as we are—capable of good, a source of learning, a link to others, and possessing an important story. With such a positive and inclusive attitude, we are prepared to learn how to begin to engage in collegial listening. *Collegial spiritual listening is an ability to attend to the whole person: body, mind, and spirit. It demands we be silent and listen to silence; we hear the words the other utters as valuable; we see the actions that person makes as conveyers of meaning; we honor the thoughts he or she expresses as sacred to him or her. It demands we honor his or her ideas as well as feelings.* Such an attitude, and the skills that accompany it, are always essential to a happy and successful life.

How to Write about Your Spiritual Life

The first thing you have to decide before writing is how, where and when you will write and whether you wish to share it. These may seem like trivial questions, but they are not. Your answer to them determines the mood you will set, whether you will be able to read what you write, and a certain consistency throughout the process that will enable you to go back and forth in your dialogue with yourself. You may modify your answers to those questions, but an initial response will get you started.

How are you going to write this autobiography? Pen, pencil, ballpoint, paper, typewriter, computer? You may feel more intimate and reflective with a pen and paper. In true journal style, you may wish to divide a paper page into four longitudinal parts with headings such as questions (date), reflection, connections (patterns), and observations. The page may be part of a bound journal of some sort. You may wish to write in the margins of this book and go back later to gather what they think is important. Maybe you are more accustomed to Twitter, Facebook, and blogs, and may want to create a log of observations on which you will later go back and reflect and seek patterns. How you are going to do this *is* important.

As a part of making decisions about how you are going to write your autobiography (diary), I strongly suggest that once you have written something, you leave it written. You may disagree with it later—even a moment later—but leave it there. Sometimes a momentary impression may fit into something you will be able to connect with later in your writing. Also, don't worry about spelling and grammar. Don't worry about erasing. Write it down. By doing so, it becomes part of your lifelong conversation.

When are you going to write it? Ideas and impressions come to us at many odd moments. They cannot be controlled. You may think you will remember what you want to write, but many times it will just slip through your consciousness. Gone. You might want to put a pen and paper next to your bed, because you may think of something on the edge of sleep that you want to write down. For all the serendipitous promptings you may have, it is always useful to put yourself on your calendar for a certain time to look at what you have written. The amount of time is also important— three minutes may seem like an eternity when you are just beginning or a fleeting moment three years from now. Perhaps you wish to start with five minutes each day, entering and looking over what you have written. Right now, here or in a notebook of some kind, write when you will do your writing and for how long. Once you're done, we can continue.

Where are you going to write? This may be unique to you. Maybe you wish to dictate while riding in your car and put it into your computer later; maybe your time alone in the lavatory is a proper place. Where is a good place to write and reflect? You may have to try a few locations before settling the best one.

A Dialectical and Dialogical Reading of Your Spiritual Autobiography

Dialectical thinking pays attention to the opposite of an idea we may hold in high regard. The implicit belief in such thinking is that out of the positive and the negative something will come that will benefit all. My two-year-old son taught me this in a humorous way. I was in the basement working when I heard a giggle and a plop sound coming from the kitchen. I stopped my work and listened more intently. Plop. Giggle. "Not a ball!" Plop. Giggle. As I came up the steps and looked into the kitchen (plop, giggle, "Not a ball!), I realized that he had opened the eggs my wife had placed on the table after shopping and, in true dialectical fashion, was learning that eggs were not balls. Lessons learned both for his parents—never leave the eggs within reach of a young child—and for him—eggs are not balls.

We learn a great deal about ourselves by looking at those who dislike us or whom we dislike. Dialogical reading is like that: negative responses may be as helpful as positive ones. For example, how would you describe a life that is not spiritual? In how many ways is your spirituality not like anyone you know? What is your future like if you don't change?

At times our ideas, practices, and ways of life may seem contradictory. Through reading, thinking, living, entering into conversations with people, exploring ideas, and learning about other ways of life, we enter into dialogue with them. Of course, an everlasting dialogue partner is the "you" who lived your past, your present, and your possible future. In reading this book, you will awaken many past experiences and possible futures. Your responses to these dialogue partners provide direction for your spiritual journey.

Most of our lives are quite ordinary. We talk. Sing. Read. Watch TV. Think. We repeat certain actions over and over to deal with the day's routine: drink water with a certain hand, get out of bed a certain way, and dress according to a certain process. We act in ways we think right. Usually we sense when we are doing wrong. We interact with people we feel close to. Every life has its habitual words, actions, and relationships that are ordinary because they are repetitive and habitual.

Living our spiritual life is usually ordinary, or habitual. It is the art of affirming or choosing the good habits that make up our spiritual life. Sometimes, though, our life is extraordinary. We experience a thing or person that deepens or draws us beyond the ordinary habits of daily living. We swim in an ocean of paradoxes and mystery. Sometimes we fall in love, or we engage in a creative task, or we share thoughts and desires. Sometimes it is an ideal, an overwhelming conviction of truth, or an experience of beauty. These moments or periods of life that draw us beyond our ordinary routine energize our ordinary life with a deepened sense of purpose and a glow of the extraordinary while being ordinary. As we stretch to become "more," our life becomes more spiritual.

Sometimes in reading our autobiography, we see that we have changed a great deal during a certain period. Life becomes extraordinary without our knowing it. Sometimes, too, we are very much aware when our life changed for a few moments, hours, days, or weeks.

I remember a young woman who participated in a workshop I was directing. One task for the participants was to walk the nearby beach and then report to the other participants their experiences. She recounted slowly walking the beach and feeling the gentle lap of the waves on her feet. Without thinking, she glanced at the telephone poles and the lines connecting one to the other. She gave in to the urge to allow her hands to stretch out toward them. She realized that, unlike them, she was connected to people but nothing went through her. She felt nothing from her relationships. This was, indeed, an extraordinary moment.

The extraordinary may be an affirmation of our spiritual life or an invitation to begin one or to abandon or modify the one we lead. Reading this book may be one of these, some of these, or all of these. To live a spiritual life, you must be aware of what you consider spiritual and what you consider valuable. You also must have an idea of what direction you wish to take in leading such a life. Dialogue and dialectic help provide this direction.

Summary

Take a breath. We all breathe. Anyone who breathes is spiritual. It is never a question of whether you are spiritual or not but of who you are spiritually. Quite early in the development of Christianity, and thus Western culture, the answer to the question of who you are spiritually was answered by saying you were a saint—you were energized by God, the Holy Spirit. Fourteen hundred years later, by the end of the Middle Ages, this primitive, wholistic mode of responding to the question had become more philosophical, dividing spiritual life from everyday life. A spiritual life was a contemplative life. You developed your spiritual life by abstaining from bodily pleasures such as sex, food, and interaction with others. You abstained from the material to direct your entire self to the nonmaterial, such as heaven, God, and things of the mind. The spiritual life was no longer for everyone. It was for the elite: nuns, monks, priests, and clergy. It was special. It was holy. It was separate from family, work, play, and the ordinary humdrum of life. It was out of this ordinary world and headed for the extraordinary, supernatural next one.

We now live in a culture that is pluralistic, global, freedom loving, and individualistic. Its understanding of spirituality reflects that culture. Spirituality seeks personal betterment and quick life changes, and transformations of the foundational challenges of life (birth, death, marriage, personal relationships, and self-image) into nonthreatening events capable of sustaining continual development toward a better life. It is independent of religions that were the traditional home of every spirituality. Today, a spirituality may be part of a classical religion or a marginal religion, or it may be independent of all religions. Today it is also part of a consumer society in which people feel free to choose a spirituality independent of peer, familial, and ecclesial pressure. To choose is to be free.

These three views of spirituality (primitive, medieval, and contemporary) are found on the Internet and in print, and are promoted by diverse celebrities. Common to all these views is that spirituality offers a promise of a transformed life and the means necessary to bring this promise to fulfillment in oneself and society. This is the understanding we will work with throughout this handbook.

To develop your spirituality and talk with others about it, you must be able to understand the language of spirituality and listen to how people, including yourself, express their spirituality. To listen to the other and to write about your spirituality involves you in a dialogical and dialectal process. It is dialogical because it brings you into a conversation with multiple partners. It is dialectical because it is a never-ending conversation with your past, present, and future—a conversation that shows you your spiritual path and puts you in contact with those with the same desire to transcend their present lives. It's also dialectical because it enables you to recognize what you do not want to become.

Dear Diary I

Where Is My Spiritual Home?

Home is a word that stimulates a diversity of emotions and memories in all of us. Some of these are positive; others, negative. Your thoughts and feelings about a spiritual home resonate with some of the same emotions surrounding the home or homes you have lived in up until the moment you read these words.

Your goal in this first "Dear Diary" is to remember, reflect, and connect your thoughts and feelings surrounding your home(s). These questions act only as stimulants. You may include your own questions and reflections either here or in another journal. Remember, the purpose of this diary, or autobiography, is to bring you into conversation or dialogue with your past and present experiences and your hopes for the future. The headings for each column provide categories for organizing your thoughts and provide a means of returning to them to reconnect what you have written with other thoughts and experiences. Here is what each heading means.

Questions—stimulants for bringing to consciousness necessary ideas and feelings for developing your spirituality.

Reflections—your response to the questions. It's best to write the first word or image that comes to mind; do not hesitate to leave the space blank and return to it later.

Connections—how your observations, reflections, and connections are related to each other. Sometimes you will leave this blank the first time you look at your response to the question.

Observations—your summary of what you have learned from your reflection and connection. Many times your observation becomes a stimulant for further reflections and connections.

You will find your own rhythm for responding to these questions. You may need another way of storing your responses beside these pages.

Questions	Reflections	Connections	Observations
What is your • age? • gender? • income? • ZIP code? • number of rooms in your present home? • make and age of your car?			
Look at your driver's license or identity card. Write the three most important pieces of information that identify you.			

Questions	Reflections	Connections	Observations
If you have a key ring or some other way of entering your important places, take it out and choose the three most important keys. Why are they important?			
Divide your age into seven-year increments. For each time period Write down your most vivid memory • Sketch the home you lived in for each period. What one room, or part of a room, in each house do you remember as especially happy? For example watching TV or sitting at the kitchen table.			

Questions	Reflections	Connections	Observations
What decisions have you made about the when, where, and how of writing this dialogical spiritual autobiography?			
Describe your birth family: sisters, brothers, position of birth, mother, father and anyone else such as stepparents.			
Any favorites among those in your family?			
Name one positive and one negative thing you inherited from each of your immediate family members.			
What families are you responsible for?			
How to they influence you?			
How long have you lived at your present residence?			

Questions	Reflections	Connections	Observations
Do you intend to remain in this general area as long as you can?			
Are there any connections between the places you have lived in the past and where you are right now?			
Are there any places you wish to be?			
Is "home" somewhere you wish to be?			
You have already described "home" as a physical place, describe it now as a community with whom you lived/live. • How many people? • Who did/do you like? • Dislike? • Could/can you speak easily with every one?			

Questions	Reflections	Connections	Observations
Are there any questions about your personal history (past) that you would like an answer to??			
How much does your past influence your present?			
Do you think your life can have a clear, achievable goal?			
Should the future influence how you act now?			
Are questions about past, present, and future useless because all that matters is what happens here and now?			
From what you have written so far, write one word that best expresses your favorite			

Questions	Reflections	Connections	Observations
• song • belief • game • holiday • way of treating others • group/community you like to be with.			
Did you ever come close to being killed?			
Do you organize things and people, or are you organized by things and people?			
Who are the people who give you a sense you are important?			
What or who determines what happens during your twenty-four-hour existence?			
If it were possible to change your past in some way, what would that change be? Name three.			

Questions	Reflections	Connections	Observations
Describe someone who leads a spiritual life. List three characteristics of someone who does not consciously lead a spiritual life?			
Does your life share any of those characteristics?			
Name four things you would want to change in your life.			
Which feelings have you experienced in your life up to this moment that are identified as spiritual? sacred • mysterious • holy • supernatural • duty and obedience to a cause, a community or a person. • justice			

Questions	Reflections	Connections	Observations
<ul><li>discipline</li><li>optimism</li><li>conviction that there is a power or energy beyond us that determines and directs our lives</li><li>Are there others that I have not mentioned?</li></ul>			
Which feelings would you be most comfortable with in your life that marks it, or moments within, as spiritual?<ul><li>sacred</li><li>mysterious</li><li>holy</li><li>supernatural</li><li>duty and obedience to a cause, a community or a person.</li><li>justice</li><li>discipline</li><li>optimism</li><li>conviction that there is a power or energy beyond us that determines and directs our lives</li></ul>			

Questions	Reflections	Connections	Observations
• Are there others that I have not mentioned?			
Some writers say you can talk only about a totally transcendent world in negatives. For example, heaven does not have clouds; God does not have human feelings. Do you agree?			
Other writers say we can talk about that which is totally transcendent using words, songs, and art that tell us something about that other world. For example, heaven is a place where God is; God became a human being. What do you think?			
Do you have a spiritual home?			

Questions	Reflections	Connections	Observations
Describe the spiritual home you would wish to have in the future.			
Is your spirituality something you find easy to talk about?			
Is there anyone with whom you can talk about your spiritual life?			
Do you think that the more spiritual someone becomes, the more he or she will talk about it?			
Is it easy to know who is spiritual and who is not?			
Do you want to deepen your spirituality?			
How much time during the day should you consciously devote to deepening your spirituality?			

Questions	Reflections	Connections	Observations
Are there any dreams that keep repeating?			
Who and/or what makes you feel • Loved • Hopeful • Empowered to persevere in living a good life.			

CHAPTER TWO

THE FOUNDATION OF YOUR SPIRITUAL LIFE

Recognizing the World of Mystery and Habit

What we do not know limits us. Life's unknowns are life's limit. No human knows everything. Every human is limited. *Mystery* is the word we use to describe both ignorance and the unknown. Our habits both free us and restrict us. They free us because their routine enables us to perform patterned actions and thoughts that provide security in everyday life. To constantly rethink whether to get up on the right or left side of the bed, eat with a fork or spoon, or drive on the left or right side of the road is confusing, to say the least. At the same time, habits restrict us and leave us ignorant of happenings in our everyday life. When our language has only a few words for snow, we cannot experience it as the Inuit do—with their many names for it; when we always wear shoes, we cannot feel the variety of terrain we walk on; when we always drink soda, we are ignorant of the benefits of drinking water. Mystery and habit are essential to living.

Spiritual Mystery

Some look at spirituality as a way to escape this present life; others, as a way to engage it more deeply. In either case, the present day, minute, and second is where and when life as we know it is lived. The past is done; the future is not yet. This present is hemmed in not only by being neither past nor future but also by being a place: we cannot be there when we are here.

Yet even in the here and now, we are severely limited to the boundaries of our sight, our hearing, our touching, our smelling, and our tasting. Our present consciousness, provided by our senses, is our glory and our limit.[7] We know there is more time than the present and more space than here. We know there is more than what our senses provide. And this "more to life" is the deep mystery of life itself. This mystery envelopes us and binds us all together in its unknowns, in its all-inclusiveness, in its boundary marking of our unique limitations.

Every spirituality is born out of the realization of personal limitation and the desire to go into that mysterious unknown that exists beyond the present limits of the here (present place) and the now (present moment). It begins with the question more felt than spoken: "Is this it?" Is this place I stand upon; these people I'm connected to; this moment of remembrance and consciousness; these feelings of joy or of guilt; these sights, sounds, touches, tastes, and smells—are these it? Is this life?

Each of us experiences these physical, mental, and social limits in our own unique way. It may be that we cannot concentrate as we would wish. We are easily distracted. It may be we have a hard time making friends. It may be we cannot walk. It may be our life is boring. It may be we are hungry and tired at the moment. It may be we cannot find the correct words to express ourselves. It may be we easily hurt others. All these "may bes" make us who we are. To recognize life's mystery and life as mystery is the beginning of discovering our spirituality.

Spiritual Habits

We are our habits. How we walk, speak, eat, think, pray, hate, love, hear, see, touch, and feel are the result of our habits. These, and so many more, were gradually initiated and learned by conscious choice or by subconscious imitation as we mimicked the habits of significant others in our life.

Spiritual habits constitute the whole range of spirituality and religion: words, actions, and community; doctrine, ritual, morality, and polity. Within this range of habits, we find two clear types of spiritual habits: *worldly* and *otherworldly*. In this case, *world* refers to everything we sense and the four dimensions of length, depth, width, and time.[8] A *worldly spirituality is one that promises and promotes individual and social transformation to a well-described future world through clearly designed processes for getting there.* For example, one may suffer from chronic depression. The clear goal is to rid oneself of its debilitating effects. The means of achieving this is a complex mix of medication and behavioral therapy.

An *otherworldly spirituality promises and promotes individual and social transformation to a metaphorically described way of life through processes warranted by spiritual authorities based on this worldly but not otherworldly reason and experience.*[9] An example of this is a type of Christian spirituality that offers heaven as its goal and the Bible as the sole authoritative means of thought, ritual, moral action, and community to achieve this goal. The authorities that provide the powerful metaphorical vision of the goal and means to it are usually recognized as these three: *tradition* as found in what we describe later as signposts (for example, rituals, beliefs, morals, and community); someone else's or one's own *transformative experience* (for example, one experiences a deep feeling of calm and an ability to foresee the future); and *thoughtful reasoning* about life's mystery. Recognizing the spiritual habits we are most comfortable with aids in knowing our present spirituality; acknowledging the necessary spiritual habits to deepen our spirituality is the beginning of changing our present spirituality.

Recognizing Spiritual Complexity and Paradox

Paradoxes are part of life. Recognizing the paradoxes inherent in life's mystery and our unrecognized habits are essential for making the choices necessary to live a healthy spiritual life. What a paradox actually is, written or otherwise, is debatable. Common to the debate is an acceptance that while being filled with absurdity and perhaps contradiction, a paradox holds its various parts together in such a way that we sense something about it is true. It brings harmony and balance out of chaos and seeming contradiction.

A paradoxical person is filled with contradictory qualities that should destroy him or her, but they do not. A paradoxical event is one that has no rational explanation while leaving us wondering how it happened. A paradoxical picture is both a rabbit and an old woman or a stairway going up and going down. A paradoxical sound seems to contain silence and sound that should cancel each other out but instead provide us with beautiful music.

A paradoxical experience leaves us convinced of its really having happened and with mixed feelings of curiosity, avoidance, attraction, repulsion, and fear. We feel it's absurd to even think it's real because one part negates the other.[10] In some instances, especially of repeated paradoxical events demanding our response, we are left with a mixture of negative and positive feelings: negative feelings of frustration, anxiety, and sometimes psychologically dangerous impulses;[11] and positive feelings of curiosity, well-being, or amazement. Sometimes we are strongly inclined to favor one part of the paradox rather than the other. The negative feelings are too intense. The seeming irrationality fills us with too much fear. We abandon the stress-filled paradox for one of its parts. In doing so, we embrace the simplicity of clear and precise answers and reject the messiness of reality. The feeling of certitude becomes more important than the search for the real.

Spiritual paradoxes produce the same effect as ordinary paradoxes by expanding our horizons and opening us up to the possibilities of new ways of living. These paradoxes have been part of living a spiritual life for thousands of years.

Here are the paradoxes that face us as we begin to describe and interact with spiritualities:

- *I am an immortal who dies.* Ernest Becker, in his Pulitzer Prize-winning book *Denial of Death* describes the paradox inherent in all human spirituality. We are angels who defecate.[12] This "angelic" nature is a conviction that we are immortal heroes. And that is the paradox: how can we be limited (dead, done in by the forces that surround us) and unlimited (immortal, capable of overcoming these forces) at the same time?

- *I need a "we" to be a "me."* Caught up in the need to discover and enhance a life of our own, we slowly come to the realization that we need others to communicate, support, and share our seekings and discoveries. We need them to share our successes and failures. We need them for approving or disapproving our style of life. We need them for food, warmth, and information. Our belly button proclaims we need others to be born. Our eyes and ears face outward, demonstrating that we need the sight and sound of others to be who we are. Somehow we grow in our unique spiritual life by a necessary sharing with others. What we especially share is a desire to make our life better than it is here and now. We wish to transcend the moment and transform our lives. Somehow "I" want to go beyond the "we," yet I need the "we" to live. Those seeking to lead a spiritual life desire to become more than they are when at midlife; more than they are in this town at this time of history; more than they are at this moment of their spiritual life. Yet they can do so only with the aid of others.

- *To be alive, I must change and remain the same.* When you look at pictures of yourself taken over the years, how can you be sure you are the same person in each of those pictures? Most people say you are the same person. Every spirituality agrees with them. Every spirituality also has a way of describing what there is about us that does not change and what does. A spirituality must do so because transcendence means change, and the transcendence which is death challenges spiritual authorities to explain how we remain the same as our body disintegrates.

- *I am one and many.* The image, definition, and nature of a human being differ among spiritualities.[13] At the minimum, they all accept that a human right now, at this place and time, is whole yet of many dimensions. In English: We are body and soul. We are mind, will, and emotions. We are, as current research and academic divisions remind us, our psychology, sociology, physics, chemistry, anthropology, and politics. No matter what the parts or dimensions we use to describe and analyze humans and their destiny, we are always a unique whole. We are one and many at the same time—something more than our individual dimensions. We are, as reminded in our first paradox, a reality that grows and disintegrates; in our second paradox, unique and interdependent; in our third paradox, still and changing.

- *My spiritual life is both free and earned, gift and purchased.* When talking about spiritualities in an American context, we sometimes are under the misapprehension that a spirituality is something we earn. "Work at it, and you will get it." "Pull yourself up by your spiritual boot straps in ten simple spiritual steps." "If you believe strong enough it will happen." Spirituality, though, as life itself, is part of the paradox of gift and purchase. Our future life is both deserved and undeserved; gift and merit. As the founder of an important Christian spirituality said, "Pray as if everything depended on God. Act as if everything depended on you."[14] As always with paradoxes, you can find many spiritualities uneasy with this saying, and thus they dissolve the paradox through belief, action, or community.

- *I must fight to be in harmony with all.* "Virtue stands in the middle" (*In medio stat virtus*) is an ancient saying that proclaims that the virtuous life is the moderate life, a life balanced between extremes. Faith itself may be seen as a continuous striving to keep one's balance between doubt and absolute truth.[15] Total doubt in one's way of life leads to personal anarchy. Total conviction of its absolute truth leads to a type of factual and experiential certitude, not faith. One loses one's balance in the extremes. While seeking balance, every spirituality calls for a total concentration of life's energies to defeat the evils inside and/or outside ourselves—all that prevent our transformation. The evils may be seen by some as evil spirits or as illusions that cause us to suffer. Still other spiritualities view the threats to our life as self-defeating habits preventing personal and social maturation. In any case, there is the paradox of keeping things in balance while attending to the all-consuming necessity to fight what unbalances us. How do we keep balanced and yet fight what unbalances us? It is like trying to ride a bike while being attacked by a helicopter.

Building a Bridge to a Transformed Life: Spiritual Sources, Signposts, and a Compass

Spiritual Sources

Anything and everything has been found to be a source of spiritual life and thus touchstones of the sacred and the transcendent. These times, places, persons, words, actions, things, and communities are believed to be a means through which we are in the presence of that power, energy, principle, or persona that sustains all existence. This presence may be a *remembered presence*, such as seeing a picture or participating in a ritual that results in recalling the power, energy, principle, or persona—much as going to a funeral and seeing a picture of the dead person might remind us of who this body was.

This presence may also be an *embodied presence*. In this instance, we believe that we are in contact with the energy and can expect to feel it coursing through our body at any moment; or in contact with our god, expect to drink his blood or to have our sins forgiven. What we see, feel, hear, touch, or taste is, for example, the words, the water, the music, the red stone. What we encounter in memory or embodiment is the foundation of our spirituality, the means of transformation, and the goal of desired transcendence. What we encounter is a source of spirituality.

Signposts of a Spiritual Life

Markers on a road provide us with the security that we are traveling in the right direction; they show us where to find the sustenance of food and drink, a place to sleep, a place for fuel, and whatever else we need for a good trip. This is a simple image of the spiritual life. If we follow the signposts, we will get where we want to go. At least that is the promise. The *inuksuk*, the signposts of those living in the Artic, are essential to the life of these people. Lacking all natural markers of where they are, since everything is flat and lifeless, they have built *inuksuk* to enable them to safely move from one place to another.

Certainly people have died or starved or lost their minds in the process that resulted in choosing the correct place for an *inuksuk*. In modern society, we many times take for granted that signposts are purely technical items easily and arbitrarily placed to direct traffic. We sometimes forget that all our signposts are in some way like the *inuksuk*. Anyone who has lived on a street where children have been killed because of improper speed limits or been lost because someone has destroyed the street signs realizes otherwise. Society constructs its *inuksuk* from its life experiences of how to travel safely from here and now to there and then.

Five signposts are found in all spiritualities. They are tangible expressions of a person and/or culture that enable us to promote our spirituality and experience the promises of transcending this current life. They are essential to any spiritual life. They vary in importance throughout our life and at each moment of our life. Belief, for example, may be more important than community at one stage of our life cycle, whereas ritual may be more important than these two at another stage. All, however, are always part of the set of signposts that provide the spiritual direction of our lives.

- *Belief* is found in stories, songs, poetry, creeds, and formal communal declarations It is expressive of a desire for truth and trust.
- *Ritual* is discovered at the sacred times of a day, week, month, year, and season. It is expressed through repeated prayers, expressions of joy, sorrow, and conviction of salvation. Whether as repeated expressions of belief combined with action or action alone, rituals express a desire for harmony and predictability of formative actions that remind us of the past and provide hope for the future.
- *Moral or ethical norms* (doing the right thing) are the communal ways of action and speech that reflect the community's view of truthful relations now and in the future:: a world of fair, loving relationships that will birth the spirituality's vision of total transformation.
- *Community* is us as we support each other's beliefs through ritual actions. It depends on each of us acting in a just and loving way toward each other. Community is reflective of a desire for togetherness, belonging, and fellow feeling.

- *Desire for transcendence* is the continually energizing force that urges us to move beyond the present to a changed future. This force, when being satisfied, is experienced as the sacred, the mysterious, the holy, the supernatural, duty, obedience to a cause, fellow feeling, belief, discipline, dedication, and/or a power or energy beyond the individual and all humans that determines and directs where and how we live. The desire for and satisfaction of transcendence is what gives value to all the other signposts.

An understanding of our spiritual signposts aids in our understanding of ourselves and the spiritual lives we develop. They all are essential for a spiritual life. A spiritual life cannot be reduced to only one of these signposts, even though some advocates for contemporary spiritualities may wish to do so. For example, saying that everything depends on one's belief and ability to project that belief into all of life enables control of outer and inner desires.

A Compass for Use in the Ocean of Paradoxes and Spiritualities

For a compass to be effective, it must have a piece of iron or steel that points north. This pointing needle enables us to know which way to direct our journey relative to the four directions: north, south, west, and east. A spiritual compass also has a needle made up not of iron but of our transcendent experiences coalescing around one root value. This "needle" enables us to direct our spiritual journey relative to the spiritual signposts (directions) embodied as root values: truth, harmony, justice, and community. Contrary to an ordinary compass, the spiritual compass's "north" varies throughout our life, while the necessary directions—or signposts, as we have called them—remain constant. Each of the points on the compass is capable of taking us in the correct direction, but we need a north to know what the true direction is for this time in our life. "North" is our pivotal root value, usually found embedded in one of the four signposts.

We recognize this root value by discovering where and how we are experiencing significant transcendence in our lives.

This *experience* of transcendence, which satiates the *desire* for transcendence, is usually stimulated and encouraged by the spiritual sources that make up the signposts. In an individual's spiritual life these sources congeal around the four values that intensify the transcendent experience: truth, harmony, justice, and community. The desire for transcendence, most intensely and continually experienced in one of these values, provides us with our spiritual direction. The rest, while present, support this enabling experience.

While these root values are not of equal importance at each moment of our spiritual lives, all must be present in a healthy spirituality. Truth, for example, may be more important than community at one stage of a life cycle, whereas harmony may be more important than these two at another point in a life cycle. All, however, are always part of the set of signposts that provide direction for our lives. All fit together with our "pointer value" taking priority and giving direction to the rest. In providing such direction, we usually see the others in the light of the pointer value. For example, when the pointer value is truth, the others (harmony, community, and justice) will be seen in the light of truth. Thus, in any of the Abrahamic religions, that would mean that no ritual is accepted unless it reflects the truth given by God in their holy scriptures. So in evangelical Christianity, which accepts only the Bible as the source of God's revelation and truth, if it's not in the Bible, it cannot be in the ritual.

The following chart is a visualization of the compass and how it acts in our life through positive and negative emotions.

A Spiritual Compass

Root *Value*	Root *Positive* Experience	Root *Negative* Experience
Truth: Belief that things are the way they should be and amazement that they are so beautiful, attractive.	It's real! I can depend on it.	Ignorance; repulsiveness
Harmony: ritual, many times resulting in a sense of well-being.	A place for everything and everything in its place.	Chaos; loss of self-control in body, mind, or spirit.
Justice: morality, doing the right thing in a fair and purposeful manner.	Action; getting things done properly.	Inertia; stasis
Community: as two individuals, love; as a group, a sense of fellow feeling and togetherness.	"We"; belonging.	Alienation; grieving for the loss of a significant other or others.

The use of the compass in our spiritual lives enables us to do three things: solidify our present sources of transcendence, recognize the role past sources play in our present lives, and discover those necessary sources of transcendence as we continue to grow in our spiritual lives. Many times the negative root experiences are more telling than the positive ones. We might easily be able to cope with being alone and alienated, yet panic when we cannot understand something or are unable to satisfy our curiosity. Our compass more than likely is pointing to truth as the primary root value. Sometimes we find that the only reason we continue to practice the religion that gave birth to our spirituality is because we feel a deep sense of joy and well-being as we celebrate the holidays or repeat prayers we were taught in our youth. Thus harmony is the value.

Our ability to know where our spiritual north is today enables us to recognize more easily what it was that provided us with a sense of identity and spiritual security in the past. If our socialization process was successful, we experienced the elation associated with the approval of authority figures as we did the right things, thought the right thoughts, and celebrated in approved ways. With time, we usually abandon some of these practices. Knowing where we are today enables us to recognize some possible sources for guilt associated with this abandonment as well as to remember the sense of well-being associated with successfully following our pointer value.

As we grow older, one of these directions becomes the dominant force in our lives. We respond to the positive experience of this root value in a stronger way than the others. Perhaps it is our sense of truth and belief that provides us with a strong sense of transcendence and becomes a means of transforming our world. We like to think and figure things out. We don't like the unknown. But, then, it may be a feeling of being together with others, or one other in married love. We don't like feeling alone and isolated from everyone else (alienation) and fear deeply the loss of a relationship to an idea, things, or a person (grief). Our needle points to our present course in relationship to possible other courses. We should take advantage of this present awareness and, realizing that the past experiences of transcendence are past, take the means to deepen the experiences that our pointer value indicates while seeking to discover its presence in the other root values.

Growing Our Spiritual Life

Every spiritual life provides a bridge between our past and present to the future. Every spiritual life provides the signposts to guide us to the future, to place us in contact with the necessary sources of spiritual energy that help us walk that bridge. The bridge stretches over our habits and the mystery of life itself to transform us and the lives of those who surround us.

"Dear Diary II" will help you become sensitive to your present spirituality. Chapters Three and Four will help put your spirituality in dialogue with those that surround you. Through dialogue and dialectic, you will walk that bridge and be transformed.

Summary

We are limited in many ways. To recognize our limits is to recognize the necessity of going beyond them—to transcend the here and now of our life. Every spirituality promises us that we can transcend our limits and provides the necessary means to do so. Habits are our everyday adaptation of our spirituality's means of transformation. But recognizing our nonreflective habits and adopting the necessary spiritual ones is the work of a lifetime of paradox and clarity. The clarity is found in the signposts and sources that enable us to encounter future transcendence in the here and now. They enable us to become involved with the sacred. The paradox is the everyday walking of our spiritual path. Our spiritual compass assures us of our current direction on that path.

DEAR DIARY II

WHAT DO I NEED TO GROW A SPIRITUAL LIFE?

Gardeners know that growing something demands total care for what's being grown, sensitivity to changes during the growth cycle, and good seeds or plants. Even though spiritual literature is filled with images of paths, roads, and pilgrimages, the idea of a garden is also included in spiritual literature. Although all those images may be beneficial in your spiritual development, I suggest that you treat your spiritual life as a growing, developing, maturing plant or animal. So much of our world sees us as machines and treats us as such that we may forget that we are not machines but living beings in need of total care and sensitivity to our changes.

What follows are questions that will stimulate your memory and challenge your willingness to grow your spiritual life. These questions, written in the spirit of Chapter Two, help you think about the structure of your spiritual life—the necessity of clarifying it and encouraging its healthy growth.

Questions	Reflections	Connections	Observations
Do you have a word for life's mystery?			
Do you think your spirituality is this worldly or other-worldly?			

Questions	Reflections	Connections	Observations
Write "true" or "false" next to the following statements. • I am an immortal who dies. • I need a "we" to be a "me." • To be alive I must change and remain the same. • I am one and many. • My spiritual life is both free and earned; gift and purchased. • I must fight to be in harmony with all.			
In reviewing the above paradoxes, underline the words and/or phrases in each statement you think best expresses your present life challenges.			
Can you live with paradox?			
Do you find life confusing: sometimes, often, always?			

Questions	Reflections	Connections	Observations
Do you feel your national culture encourages the following feelings? Write "yes" or "no." well-being • connecting with everything (animate and inanimate) that surrounds you • the people and technocracies that surround you are truthful and trustful • fellow-feeling; togetherness • following one's purpose and direction in life			
Prioritize the following words according to your present feelings (use 1 for the most important; 5 for the least.) • Pain • Loss • Ignorance • Alienation • Purposelessness			

Questions	Reflections	Connections	Observations
Provide a one-word description of • body • soul • spirit			
Does using words like *soul* and *spirit* help you understand life's mystery?			
Are you able to think of a spiritual life without dividing the person into body, soul, and spirit?			
Do you have an image of your final transformation? For example, heaven or enlightenment or perfect peace and prosperity?			
Is there another world(s) we could live in addition to this earth? Where is it? When is it?			
What is your body's relationship to this world? Is it up there? Inside you? Beside you?			

Questions	Reflections	Connections	Observations
Is it at the end of this world? At a specific moment in the future?			
A spiritual life must include which of the following? Mark "yes" or "no." If in doubt, mark "no." the community as of central importance • the individual as of central importance • no interference from political powers or law • easily understood beliefs • A special book where everything may be found for leading a spiritual life • an experienced spiritual leader for all who wish to live this way of life • a god or God • a clear indication of what will prevent you from leading a spiritual life • clearly indicated days and times when rituals associated with the spiritual life should be practiced			

Questions	Reflections	Connections	Observations
Which of the following are—or you would like to be—your spiritual sources? • certain people • ideas • community • ways of action • books • songs • holidays • required ways of acting • Other?			
Does *spiritual* in the above have a specific reference? For example, God, Tao, or Brahman.			
Which religion, if any, did you practice in your preteens?			
Do you remember any times, places, people, or things within that religion that were a particular source of spiritual devotion or fear?			

Questions	Reflections	Connections	Observations
Briefly describe your spiritual signposts: • beliefs • rituals • ethical norms • community in which you live your spiritual life			
Looking back at your spiritual signposts, write how often you practiced each of them this last week.			
Is the spiritual life you have just described important to you?			
The following is a description of what is known as "American" religion. Answer yes or no to each statement. My spirituality • is able to be understood by others • has a personal God • enables me to speak to God • has rituals, the best of which are spontaneous, joyful, and make me feel better when completed			

Questions	Reflections	Connections	Observations
• has clear moral standards • has standards based on the Ten Commandments • It's my conscience that tells me what's right and wrong, not a church or government. • It would be wrong for a government or a church to force me to join it. • If I join or am a member of a religion, I want the leader of that religion to be deeply spiritual. • That leader should be a good preacher, capable of making me feel spiritual. • I am convinced that there is a super-natural world com-posed of spirits. • The spirits in this world are all good. • The spirits in this world are good (want to help me) and bad (want to hurt me).			

Questions	Reflections	Connections	Observations
• My spirituality has a special day to gather with those who share my spirituality. • My spirituality does not have many traditions. • An important part of my spirituality is that it makes me feel good and energized for healthy living. • Religions are best when they can compete among themselves by offering us what we need.			
Look back at the spiritual compass described in Chapter Two. Arrange in order of priority how you feel right now regarding the negative experiences (ignorance, chaos, boredom, alienation). Arrange in order of priority how you feel right now about the positive values (truth, harmony, justice, community).			

Chapter Three

The Classical Spiritualities

Up to this point in your search, your spirituality has been the center of the discussion. Your past and present have been the focus of your dialogue and dialectic. With this and the next chapter, you will be offered a chance to come into dialogue with the spiritualities that surround you.

The ideal would be that you gather regularly with those who live these spiritualities. If you are fortunate enough to have an interfaith dialogue group, what I have to say in these chapters and your responses to the "Dear Diary" questions will be enlivened by how these spiritualities are lived day by day, decade by decade. This chapter offers contrasting views of how the classic spiritualties understand the person, death, and suffering. "Dear Diary" offers you an opportunity to bring your signpost into dialogue with those of the classic spiritualities. A summary of the classic spiritualities can be found in appendix B, "Key Facts for Classic Spiritualities." This is a quick review of everything we say in this chapter.

A spirituality, as I have suggested, is a way of life seeking a beneficial transformation and transcendence of self and community. A spiritual life promises and promotes the vision and means to change the present world into another world in the near or distant future. Both vision and means are culturally dependent. The shift in pivotal means is expressed in the spiritual north indicated by your spiritual compass. The "American religion" I brought you into dialogue with at the end of "Dear Diary II" is an example of a spirituality that has influenced you positively or negatively. To study spiritualities, we divide them into easy categories for analysis. These categories can aid us in the practical task of discerning our own spirituality and how it may grow in the future.

This chapter brings you into dialogue with those spiritualities that have stood the test of time, established the foundation of current world cultures, enlivened the lives of billions of people, and left humanity with invaluable ideas, music, stories, architecture, and other works of art and thought. There are many ways to describe them. A few categories may be helpful in getting us started. These are descriptions based on your geographical location, on your understanding of God, and your view of history. No category encompasses everything it hopes to describe, nor should it ever become a way of judging individuals. Categories are constructs that help us understand our life and our world. Here are a few that might be helpful.

Western and Eastern Spiritualties

A common way of talking about world religions and world spiritualities is to look at them from the perspective of the European scholars who first studied comparative religion. They divided the world into Eastern religions (Hinduism, Buddhism, Confucianism, Taoism [Daoism], Shinto) and Western religions (Judaism, Christianity, Islam). Appendix B provides a summary of the signposts for each of these spiritualties.

Western

Judaism originated in 1200 BCE; Christianity in 30 CE; Islam in 609 CE. Among the classic religions, these are not the oldest. They represent 53.7 percent of the world's population (Christianity, 33.1 percent, Islam,

20.4 percent, Judaism, 0.2 percent). They are the majority in 154 nations (Christianity in 106, Islam in 47, Judaism in 1).[16] Commentators describe them as monotheistic religions, religions of the book, Western religions, and Abrahamic religions.[17] They are a formative influence on Western civilization. Many of the ideas, language, and expectations associated with spirituality of those who read and speak English as their primary language are found here. We begin with Judaism, because it is the first historically. The other Western spiritualities see themselves as somehow a clearer or more complete fulfillment of God's original covenant with the Jews.

Eastern

These religions, and the spiritualities embedded in them, are among the oldest classical religions in the world: Shinto (2000 BCE), Hinduism (1500 BCE), Buddhism (531 BCE), Confucianism (551 BCE), and Taoism (350 BCE).[18] They represent 26 percent of the world's population: Shinto, 3 million; Hinduism, 870 million (13 percent), Buddhism 380 million (5.9 percent), Confucianism, 6 million (0.1 percent) and Taoism, 3 million.[19]

Spiritualities Based on Our View of God.

Monistic spirituality envisions present, past, and future as one. All reality is unified in such a way that the promised use of the means provided by the spirituality enables the practitioner to remove the barriers that prevent him or her from realizing his or her oneness. This does not rule out the presence of gods and spirits in our present deformed state of existence. Many of these spiritualities recognize such entities as necessary beings in the human evolution to oneness. Eastern spiritualities are usually referred to as monistic.

Monotheistic spirituality envisions time as linear and history as causal of present existence. The one God who created and is creating this world is seen as the force that will bring it to perfection in the future. The means provided to us humans sets the scene for this perfecting action. There is only one God. Any other gods, spirits, animate and/or inanimate realities depend on God for their existence. The Western spiritualities are understood to be monotheistic and may be described as dualistic, since creator and created can never be one.

Polytheist spirituality may exist within a cyclical, linear, or unified view of time. This world, and any possible evolutions of it, results from the interaction of gods and spirits with the one we see, feel, and hear. The power of a god or spirit is unique to each god or spirit, yet it is usually envisioned within a hierarchy of gods. Eastern spiritualities are seen to be polytheistic. Western spiritualities may also be seen as polytheistic when spirits of all sorts, such as angels and devils, are part of that spirituality and God is seen as one among many powerful good and bad spirits.

Atheistic spirituality is usually defined by what it rejects: an all-powerful and knowing creator, God. In contemporary culture, it is often understood by its adherents to be the total adherence to the promise promoted by scientism and the means of perfection offered by the sciences.

Agnostic spirituality promises and promotes an ability to live wholistically in the midst of acknowledged continual uncertainty as to human betterment and positive change. Many times such agnosticism is seen as essential for living in liminal times.

Spiritualities Based on Longevity and Adaptability.

Classical spiritualities share the longevity and signposts of the classical religions. While the past is no predictor of the future, the spiritualities' ability in the past to change while remaining the same suggests they will evolve to live beyond these liminal times. Their greatest challenge, however, will be in their ability to transform those aspects of their promises and promotions tied to one culture and still be recognized as the same. The current seeming necessities of environmentalism, pluralism, and gender equality are special challenges to such identity of culture and spirituality.

- *Western classical spiritualties* are those spiritualities that find their origin in religions of Judaism, Christianity, and Islam.
- *Eastern classical spiritualties* are those that find their origins in the religions of India (Hinduism, Buddhism, Jainism, Sikhism) and of East Asia (Taoism, Shinto, and Confucianism).
- They share in a common transcendent desire and the necessity of all five signposts. They differ significantly regarding their sense of time, deity, and humanity.

Marginal spiritualities express the vision of those who have rejected the classical spiritualities throughout history. Their language and imagery sometimes reflect that of ancient oral cultures and at other times the experiences and oratory of contemporary charismatic personalities. Most contemporary marginal spiritualities are composites of visions and signposts picked from ancient writings and imbued with contemporary language that titillates one's transcendent desires. Today synonyms for marginal spiritualities are sects, cult, occult, new age, esoteric, mystical, or metaphysical.

Me, Our World, and My/Our Spirituality

Many contemporary discussions of spirituality begin with the individual and his or her life. The classical spiritualities each offer a view of the individual, an individual's life, and the world that she or he participates in. As you read what follows, bring your spirituality into dialogue with those of the classical spiritualities. The result should be a clarification of the ideas behind your spirituality. Such clarification should also enable you to affirm the signposts that will help transform your life.

This "world" that we live in was described in Chapter One as Life's Mystery. Let's imagine we are fish in an aquarium. Life's mystery would be everything that is part of our present life: the here and now of all our senses, of our mind, of our soul, of our spirit. As with the fish, what makes up our here and now (the aquarium and everything in it) is both part of who we are and the limit of who we are. An important experience in growing up is recognizing what is not me (the aquarium and everything in it). In its own way, this is "other" than me: the water, the aquarium walls, the flora and fauna, the other fish in the aquarium with me. Each spirituality deals with this relationship of the self and others, and how we live out this relationship marks our growth in the spiritual life. Part of contemporary spiritual language in the West contains terms such as *body*, *soul*, *mind*, and *spirit*. If we are to understand who we are, these terms have to be part of that explanation.

There are four ways of understanding the self in contemporary spirituality: the self as here and now but not yet (Western), the self as neither here nor now (Eastern, Indian), the self as here and now there and then (Eastern Chinese and Japanese), the self as here and now (survival). In other words, the self is in the aquarium but destined to be out of it (West); not part of the fish or the aquarium (Eastern, Indian); part of the aquarium and whatever it becomes (Eastern: Chinese and Japanese); a fish in the aquarium (survival).

I Am Here and Now, but Not Yet

Judaism, Christianity, and Islam differ radically in many things, but are one in their belief in an eternal creator-God, that all of creation has a purpose given it by its creator, that that purpose will be fulfilled by listening to what God tells them to be and do, and that all of creation, but especially humans, have a role to play in fulfilling that purpose. When God said "It is good," this "good" included humans. Yet humans do bad things that are a result of not listening to God and that prevent them, and all creation, from becoming better. As a consequence, who they are right now is neither who they should be nor who God wishes them to be. They have further to go in their personal and interpersonal relationships. Who they are here and now will be perfected in the future. That future is described by such terms as *new world, resurrection, Kingdom of God, heaven*, and *paradise*. No matter what this future is called, God is always essential to its creation. We humans cannot do it all by ourselves.

Who am I? I am a co-creator of my individual and communal future. How do I know what to do to fulfill God's purpose? The signposts provided by my tradition offer me a guide to the unique future envisioned by my spirituality. A central one of those signposts is a book that is both unique to each spirituality yet having much in common with the books of the other spiritualities. The book shares many stories, laws, personages, and visions of their common God. For Jews, this book is the Tanakh, for Christians, the Bible, and for Muslims, the Quran. This book, and the tradition of spiritual interpretations within which it resides enables me to say yes to who I am and to who I will become. In doing so, I say yes to God.

I Am Neither Here nor Now

The varieties of Hinduism and Buddhism all calmly plead for us to stop, to be, to cease, to end this foolishness of desire that reveals our ignorance and intensifies our suffering. To remove ourselves from our past actions that have placed us in this foolish situation. To follow the sound of *om* beyond its inner origins to its true source and discover that the seeker and the one sought are the same as the speaker and the listener. There is no "here and now," no "there and then." There is no time or place. Say no to your seeking and yes to your true being. The wisdom of the tradition, sometimes reflected in the ancient writings, energizes and directs you to do this. Follow the path that fits your needs, whether it is devotion to one of the gods, experiencing true wisdom, or acting in the proper manner. Certainly your past bad acts have to be dealt with as well as your present ones. Walking the proper path, directed by those who walked it before you, will enable you to realize you have always been at both its beginning and its end. This end is described as nirvana or Brahman—an end that you are. You can do it. Others have.

I Am Here and Now; There and Then

All is in balance. All is harmonious. But today all, including you, are unbalanced and disharmonious. One act, one chance happening, one thought is enough to unbalance our lives. Balance and harmony come about when we begin, and continue, to build a perfect character that recognizes our part in the whole. We build this character by perfecting the necessary ways of acting and speaking that embody the harmonizing rituals that make us part of the whole. Foods, words, actions, interactions, breathing, and drinking—all must be in harmony. Peace, harmony, and a long life as part of an embracing community are the destiny we deserve and can achieve together with others. Our present is one with our future when all are in harmony with each other. You can be this fully mature and healthy person. Let it be.

I Am Here and Now

Survival is about food and drink, pleasure and pain, warm and cold. When life is short, distances long, and pain a constant reminder of present realities, there is not much time for reflecting on the future. The story is told of a tribe of pigmies who were brought out of their forest to a large savanna. They could not recognize distances, because distances had never been part of their experiences. To us a boat in a lake far away is a boat in a lake; to them it is a stick on a pond. When your spatial and temporal horizons change, your spirituality shifts along with them. That deep yearning to be more than you are at this moment and place is still present, matched in its own way by the stories and rituals handed down by your ancestors and the power provided by your mind, muscles, and instruments of death and life. You know you can be more than you are. But such knowledge is more hope than reality, and all the signposts direct you to perfect the here and now. In such perfecting life is good; life is longer; and pain is diminished. You live!

Body, Mind, Soul, and Spirit(s)

The principle thrust of the *Western tradition* identifies the person with all she affirms as "me." This "me" carries over into the perfected future with some consciousness of her past. One must remember that present consciousness of the past is never perfect. Often it is formulated in terms of present concerns and future expectations. Yet the Western tradition always affirms and honors the value of the present individual in the final transformation. To affirm the reality of mind, soul, and spirit is to provide hints to this final transformation, because each of these realities provides experiences beyond the here and now. They enable "the fish" to reach beyond the aquarium and provide hope of life without it.

The *Eastern tradition* affirms and honors the reality of the impersonal dynamism of the universe, whether it is Tao, Brahman, or Sunyata (nothingness). Neither mind, body, soul, nor spirit is real in the sense that this dynamism—who you are—actually exists. To speak of mind, soul, and spirit is to remind us that we are more than our senses. But as long as "you" are being reminded and "you" are experiencing, you distract yourself from who you really are. The final transformation is becoming one with this dynamism. The fish and the aquarium must disappear along with your soul, mind, spirit, and body.

The *survival tradition* sees body, mind, soul, and spirits as part of this present life. Brother Fox and Mother Earth, while highly metaphorical to present technological humans, are made very real in daily intimate relationships that result in survival. Everything and every one is part of an infinite aquarium where we swim together for the benefit of all.

Which of the above best expresses your spirituality and your ideal of where you wish to be when this life is finished by your death? The classic spiritualties have developed ways of talking about the end of this life and the beginning of the next—if there is one. Their views of death and afterlife may help you clarify your future hopes and dreams.

Death and Afterlife: A Conversation among the Classical Spiritualities

Many of the spiritual lessons about death are taught through the signposts of the classical religions. These lessons have sustained billions over the centuries as they faced death in all its multifaceted forms. Whether the symbols embedded in these signposts are adequate for our present times is a question being answered by those living these spiritualities today.

Western Culture: Christianity, Judaism, Islam

Christianity

Many descriptions of afterlife surround us. The symbols of Christian architecture, song, art, and literature express not only their original intent but also the meaning given them over the centuries. The same holds true for the center of Christian life, the Bible. The Bible was composed and compiled over two thousand years ago with parts of the Tanakh (Old Testament), which is over four thousand years old. Its portrayal of death reflects that development.

Jesus and the first generation of those who followed him were Jews born and raised in what is now Israel and Palestine at the beginning of the Common Era. As Jews, they inherited the symbols and understanding of the afterlife as present among their people. By Jesus's time there were two dominant views of afterlife: at death one enters more deeply into the history and life of the Jewish people; at death one ceases to exist but will resurrect when the world as we know it ends and the new one begins. It is important to understand the two beliefs that are inherent in these views of afterlife. One is the belief in God as creator. The only reason anything exists is because God keeps it in existence. Humans are kept alive because God keeps them alive. If we live after death, it is because God continues to create us after we die. If God chooses to do that immediately after death, at some later time (for example, the end of the world), or in some other manner than God does right now, that's God's choice, not ours.

The first generation of Jesus's followers believed that he was the first human to be resurrected—not resuscitated. In other words, after his death, Jesus was living as a human in a new bodily form. It was totally different than how he lived before he died. He was resurrected. He was not merely made alive in the same body (resuscitated). They also believed that they would be resurrected when they died and that this resurrection would happen to them at the end of time if they followed Jesus's way of life. After their death, they rested in peace until the end of the world, when they would be resurrected.

The followers of Jesus's way of life increased. Many of these followers were from another culture that surrounded the Jewish one—the Greco-Roman. This culture and its language contained the body-soul division inherent in many of the cultures of the Western world today, including English. It was not long before the followers, now called Christians, began talking about a person's body and soul. In doing so, they had to confront another idea inherent in the Greco-Roman culture: immortality. For the Greeks and the Romans, immortality meant that you were a soul. Your body was something you lived in while you did what was necessary to return to the heavens from which you came. Your soul was eternal. It was not born and did not die. For the Jews and the early Christians, God was eternal and only God could live forever. To keep their faith in God as creator and the resurrection of humans, they conceived of humans as both body and soul, as the Greeks did, but that God created both the body and soul when a person was born. Death separated the body from the soul. The body decomposed; the soul rested until resurrection.

With time the "heavens" came to be seen as the place of light and perfect materials. People also came to understand that the reality within each person that sought perfection was like light itself. The "soul" was destined to be in the heavens. Christians of the West, therefore, began to believe that when people died their soul went to heaven to be with God while their bodies decomposed in the earth. At least the souls of the Christians who followed Jesus's way went to heaven. Those souls who did not follow Jesus went to a place devoid of God—hell. At the end of the world, the church authorities stated, everyone would be resurrected and go to heaven or hell. Some theologians thought that at the end of the world only the good people would live forever. The others would not.

Over time, and the interaction of cultures with the Christian way of life, the afterlife also gained a population of angels and devils. The place of both heaven and hell also changed as people's views of the cosmos changed. At the beginning, heaven was above the clouds with mountain peaks marking some of heaven's boundaries. Then it shifted to the edge of the solar system, then to the edge of the known cosmos, and finally to a dimension beyond the senses. Some stopped talking about heaven as a place and saw it as a relationship with God that intensified as we lived our lives here on earth and then later in other dimensions. Hell, as a place, was usually seen as the opposite to the heavens, at the center of the earth—a place one could also enter through caves and volcanoes. Ultimately it, too, as a place, was posited in another dimension beyond the natural senses. It was seen as a relationship where those who rejected anything of God lived their life without God—forever.

For some Christians, especially Roman Catholics, a place, or later a relationship, called Purgatory developed. If you died falling short of changing enough to live in heaven, this place enabled you to become perfected enough to enter heaven. People spent their time in Purgatory becoming a better person until they were prepared to live with God forever. Since Christianity was seen as a community (communion of saints) who helped each other in this life, it was understood that they could help each other in the next. So people prayed, fasted, and gave money to the poor to help those in Purgatory become purified of their sins, just as they were supposed to help them in this life. Of course, this communion of saints worked the other way around: those in heaven could help those on earth. Thus, for example, the dead—saints—were prayed to for a good harvest, a healthy child, or a lost job.

Another afterlife place developed as Christian thinkers tried to understand two seemingly contradictory parts of their belief. People can enter heaven only if they are baptized and believe in Jesus and follow his way of life, and there are many good and innocent people who are not baptized. How could these people go to hell? The tentative response to this seeming contradiction was answered by the concept of Limbo. Limbo was where these good, innocent, people lived their lives apart from both God and the devil in the best possible life after death.

Christians, then, have a variety of answers to the question of their individual futures after death. Today most of them would say that their souls have an afterlife in heaven with friends and God. This afterlife is one in which a person has a memory of his life on earth as well as his life in heaven. Some of these Christians also believe they will live again as some kind of body-soul after this world ends and a new one begins—that is, resurrection. Evil people go to hell, where they suffer forever, now and after the resurrection. People go to heaven or hell depending on their knowledge of and how they follow Jesus's way of life.

Judaism

Ancient Judaism's view of the afterlife might be seen to begin with God's creation of humans when God breaths into the dust the spirit of humanity, thus creating the first human (Genesis 2:7). To the first Jews, death was when this breath of life returned to God and the dust of the ground returned to being dust. Each human was a unity of earth and spirit animated by God. Individual afterlife was not part of their mental landscape. God promises in Genesis 12:1-3, that the Jewish nation, not the individual, will live forever.

Gradually this vision of ancestral life after death develops into a personal life after death through resurrection. Initially resurrection is portrayed as the Jewish dead rising from their graves to provide an army for

69

Israel (Ezekiel 37:7-10). Then this prophetic vision is applied to all humans and their judgment at the end of time (Daniel 7). By the time of Jesus, resurrection is the dominant Jewish view of afterlife, and it becomes embedded in the culture with the destruction of Jerusalem (70 CE). This literal view of our bodies returning to life is a seed for further development over the next two millennia.

These ancient views of afterlife are retained among contemporary Jews within a culture that sees the human person as a composite of body-soul. Some Jews say our afterlife is found in how our children and our children's children remember us. Others say we will resurrect at the end of the world. Still others claim our soul lives forever with God, and there is no such thing as bodily resurrection.

Islam

Islam begins and ends with the oft-repeated proclamation "There is no god but Allah, and Muhammad is his prophet." Allah causes life, death, and afterlife (Surah 22:66). Islam shares with both Judaism and Christianity the dominant view of afterlife in its original, seventh-century, culture: bodily resurrection. It also shares the common challenge to the belief in bodily resurrection: what happens to the person while she or he waits for resurrection to happen? Judaism and Christianity answered the challenge in two ways. One was to say we rest (Rest in Peace) until the resurrection. Another, which accepts the body-soul view of the person, has the soul go to heaven upon death while waiting for the resurrection. The dominant view within Islam understands the rest of sleep to be a time when we return to God. It is also a time for eternal rest. Thus, when we go to sleep every night, we enter into God's world. Our death is a permanent entry into what we experience every night. We are able to communicate with those who are in eternal rest through our dreams. Upon awakening from eternal rest through the resurrection, the good will enjoy the pleasures and wonders of the afterlife; the evil will suffer the pain and torment of eternal punishment. The majority of Muslims retain these original views of afterlife contained in their holy scriptures, the Quran.

How Western Religions View God's Final Judgment of Our Life

Contemporary Western culture many times escapes responsibility for action through a scientific explanation for action. Ancient cultures, and the religions that originated within those cultures, affirmed that we are responsible for all our actions, and these actions are part of who we are. Depending on what we have done, we are a good person or a bad person. Contemporary Jews, Christians, and Muslims include in the understanding of a good person the intent and wish of that person do something good. Most Western legal systems are based on intention, willfulness, and what the person has actually done.

One religious symbol of our continuing into the afterlife as a good person or a bad person is the Judgment by God or one of God's delegates—for example, an angel. All three religions have some version of a judgment scene—either at the moment of the individual's death or at the end of the world before or after resurrection. Since the concept of "soul" did not exist in ancient Judaism, judgment was first seen in reference to the nation of Judaism being judged as it carried out its covenant duties with God. As the idea of resurrection developed, so did the concept of a judgment at the end time that resulted in either resurrection to life or damnation to destruction (Ezekiel 37:11-14; Daniel 12:1-2).

Christianity inherits and elaborates on these images of judgment from its understanding of Jesus's role as Messiah. The last book of the Christian Bible, Revelation, provides an especially vivid judgment scene and description of the place where God dwells, the heavenly Jerusalem (Revelation 21, 22). One is judged in Christianity as well as in Judaism according to how she or he has kept the covenant obligations. Of these obligations, one obligation in particular is highlighted in both religions' visions of judgment: how the nation and/or the individual care for the poor. The judgment scene in the book of Matthew in the Christian Bible perhaps summarizes this emphasis the best when it describes Jesus coming at the end of time and all the people gathered around his judgment throne. He begins to divide people according to whether they gave drink to the thirsty, food to the hungry, and clothes to the naked. Those who were rejected asked, "When did we see you like this?" and the judge, Jesus, says, "When you didn't do it for the least of those near you, you didn't do it to me" (Matthew 25).

As both Judaism and Christianity entered more deeply into a culture and language that emphasized the individual and accepted the concept of the soul, the vision of judgment at the end of the world began to be applied to the individual immediately after death. This judgment also began to reflect the dominant issues of the time. In Christianity, for example, the Ten Commandments were not central to norming the moral life for the first fifteen hundred years of the Christian tradition. Until the Protestant Reformation, the seven deadly sins were central in envisioning how people would be judged. From the sixteen century onward, the Ten Commandments held center stage. An example of this is a comparison between moral manuals used by Catholic priests between 1598 and 1716 CE. The commandments dealing with stealing, lying, and coveting cover 154 pages; those dealing with sex had four pages. God's judgment at death and resurrection, therefore, would reflect these norms, according to the priest-confessor.

Islam also has symbols associated with judgment. Both the judgment of the soul and the resurrection of the body are present within the Quran. The souls of the wicked are torn out of their bodies and questioned immediately upon death. Not recognizing God or his prophet, they are condemned to the fires of Jahannam. The good person's soul is not interrogated by the angels of death but gently released and led into the sleep of the faithful until the resurrection. According to some accounts, the good soul is led by the angels into the garden of life to await the resurrection (Surah 16:28-32). The original judgment is affirmed at the resurrection, and the consequent afterlives described as living in the garden of sensual delights for the good and the horrible tortures of Jahannam for the evil ones.

Eastern Culture: Hinduism, Buddhism, Taoism, Confucianism, Shinto

We have seen how the western classical spiritualities adapted to the Greco-Roman culture's view of the soul. There were many other ideas and ways of life that were modified as Christianity became part of the Greco-Roman culture and, later, the cultures of Europe. Similar changes happen as the non-Western cultures enter the Western world through such avenues as the English language. Four adaptations, or translations, have special consequences for discussions of afterlife in the English language: the nature of the "I" that lives in the afterlife; the relationship of the afterlife to this life; the nature of ultimate reality; the manner through which the afterlife becomes better than this life.

When those in the West ask the question "Do I exist?" they usually identify "I" with an awareness of the world around them, an ability to think, to desire, to will to do things, to remember, and to wish for a future that is beneficial to the one who is thinking, desiring, willing, and remembering. If they are members of one of the Western religions, they believe that God is somewhat like them and possesses some of these same characteristics while still being completely different. Humans are not God. As members of these religions, they believe that what they do and believe in this life affects their lives in the next; they have only the one chance of this life to prepare for the next life. Time is linear. God is totally different from humans. There is an actual afterlife with this God.

Eastern religions do not look at life or afterlife in any of the ways we described above. The "I" as such does not exist, since we are all one. The universe, both seen and unseen, is one. Time is cyclical. The Western word *God* is not applicable to ultimate reality. There is no afterlife as such; there is only this life, lived in the right or wrong way, which we live over and over until we get it right. Lived correctly, one realizes and becomes one with the universe which we are: a universe which itself is nothing (Buddhism).

In *Hinduism*, the real "I" is eternal, is divine, and actually is the universe. Everything we sense is false and leads us away from the true reality of this universe. Death, too, is a moment marking the false world we have and are creating. Everything we do creates our futures. Until we act, feel, and think correctly, we are destined to live forever, incarnate in this false world we create. Life after life, reincarnation after reincarnation, follows our inability to rid ourselves of our karma, our creation of false lives.

Only through liberating-knowledge will we discover the true nature of the world we are and break the endless cycle of birth, life, death, and rebirth. In experiencing knowledge that we are the divine, we, as conscious, sensing, thinking, willing, remembering entities cease to exist. Various types of meditation enable us to have this experiencing knowledge. Another way to stop this false existence is through the way of devotion. In this instance, we focus our attention on one of the many gods in the Hindu religion. In the *Bhagavad-Gita,* for example, Krishna promises freedom from this illusory world if we fix our attention on Krishna alone and follow his way of life.

Buddhism, with its origins in Hinduism, looks at the individual's future in much the same way: affirming the ideas of continual rebirth or reincarnation; the falsity of this world as we sense it and become attached to it; and the need to escape from this false existence. While Hinduism emphasizes that ignorance binds us to this falsity, Buddhism emphasizes that our desires create and bind us to a false mode of existence. We must extinguish all desire to be conscious, thinking, willing, remembering, and feeling. When we are nothing, we are in nirvana—saved from all craving and suffering.

Between death and re-incarnation, many other worlds exist in Hinduism and Buddhism. Some of these occur while we are dying, others immediately after death, and sometimes for long times after death—before we are reborn into this world. These worlds are populated with various beings who try to pull us into their false worlds, thus preventing us from being re-incarnated or entering nirvana.

Taoism understands ultimate reality as harmony resulting from the two complementary and interdependent forces of *yin* and *yang*: the positive and negative; being and non-being; light and darkness. Humans are one aspect of the Tao, whether alive or dead. Death is part of the everlasting harmony of the universe. Our wills, desires, memories, feelings, freedoms, and bodies do not continue beyond death. One's present life may be extended by such actions as living a moral life, regulating our eating, esoteric sexual activities, and interaction with others. Confucianism is much like Taoism in its emphasis on harmony, the extension of this life by natural means, and the denial of the soul's existence after death.

Shinto understands ultimate reality as *kami,* a spiritual force that transcends and is expressed in all things. Life is a mirror of this *kami* energy; death is its mirror opposite. It is important for one to live a life worthy of being remembered as a famous ancestor. Those who were famous enough as an ancestor would be remembered by all as worthy of becoming part of the eight hundred kinds of *kami* in the spirit world.

Hopefully, this quick survey of death in the classic spiritualities has given you opportunities to not only listen to the diverse understandings of death but also to reflect on how your death is part of your spirituality. Such a survey can easily leave out the multiple realities associated with death, such as the grief of those surrounding the dying person and the emotions coursing through the dying person herself. It can also give the impression that the deep suffering that accompanies dying and death is of little import. We cannot leave the foundational spiritual event of death and afterlife without reflecting on the role of suffering in our spirituality. Ultimately our afterlife begins in this life with its mixture of suffering, evil, and the wonderful exhilaration offered by the life around and within us.

Classic Spiritualities and the Fact of Human Suffering

Questions in Life and about Life

Every life story has its exclamation points, periods, and question marks. Here we are interested in the question marks. We ask questions about life as it happens as well as when it is over. Noticing a cut on my daughter's arm, I ask, "How did it happen?" Facing a dentist's drill, I inquire, "Will it hurt?" Getting laid off, I demand, "Why me? What did I do?"

Questions have a way of probing the world around us. They stretch to the past and probe the present to allow us to live better in the future. To know that my daughter's cut was caused by a piece of metal on her bike, that the dentist will give me something for the pain, and that everyone fifty-nine and older was let go makes a difference for future living by allowing me to plan for that future.

Some questions and answers are larger than themselves. They point to larger questions and answers than are presently available. Why do we suffer? Why do we die? Do we have a future? are questions that are never fully answered. Our attempts to answer them make a difference in the way we live our lives. These are what might be described as *making-sense questions*: questions that both when asked and when answered bring our stories together differently than when they are not asked or answered. They express the plot of a person's life story. Even to ask these questions about suffering, death, and the future is to proclaim that we know these experiences and to suggest that the world should have some purpose—otherwise, why ask? To receive an answer to these questions, no matter how tentative, suggests a plot for your own life story and that of everyone you know. To live your life with an awareness of that plot is to test both question and answer. In living the answer, it is not unusual to discover a new question—making-sense questions are like that. Once we think we know the "sense," we are anxious to know if they are non-sense.

Questions and answers are never individual questions and answers. Because we are interdependent, because our stories are part of a mutual history, questions and answers are shared. Questions and answers about suffering, death, and future are also shared. The questions you have are all part of larger communities of shared questions and answers. Over time, national, religious, philosophical, or cultural groups have developed ways of asking and answering these making-sense questions.

When we suggest large categories of thought and action, we always risk leaving someone out and/or not allowing room for mixtures of categories. Such a risk is worthwhile, however, when we are able to present paradigms that are easily understandable and useful for dealing with those who grieve and suffer. There are four famous answers to our three questions: Why do we suffer? Why do we die? Do we have a future?

Four Answers to Life's Questions

"It's absurd." Life is absurd. Death is absurd. It's absurd even to ask the question about the future, since all we know and experience is the here and now. After all, life is just one damn thing after another, so what is the use of even thinking about it?

It is of no use thinking about it, but there is a benefit to doing something about it. You prove you can beat life's absurdity. Get up in the morning and face the boredom of life, knowing that in facing it you prove you will not let its absurdity do you in. To be human and alive is to thumb your nose at the boredom, absurdity, and stupidity of life itself.

The ancient myth of Sisyphus is a good example of this response to our questions. Sisyphus was condemned to push a large boulder up an enormous mountain. Through rain, snow, sleet, cold, and hot, he strained to get the boulder to the top of the mountain. Day after day, night after night, his only goal was to push the boulder to the top. Strained muscles, scraped knees and arms, bruised shoulders and face did not stop him. Every day he pushed. Every day he inched his way to the top. Then one day he reached the top. In exultation, he paused in triumph. While he paused, the boulder rolled down the mountain. His eternity was to push the boulder to the top. His humanity was to look from the top of the mountain at the boulder below and, with shoulders square, to turn to begin again. Death? Suffering? Future? "Absurd? But damn it, I'll keep pushing!"

"That's life" is another response. Some see life as a set of immutable laws, patterns, relationships, or recognized expectations that, if broken,

result in suffering or death. The immutable laws may be titled natural, physical, or social; they may be seen as the deep and expected relationships between all beings. Whereas the "It's absurd" perspective looks at life in a negative way, this perspective may have either a positive or a negative outlook. But it is accepting of what causes the suffering or the death, because it sees all of life in a give-and-take perspective where everything must be balanced. It is enough to say that the person died of cancer or that the war was caused by people's dislike of their dictator. From this perspective, the future is determined by the present. There are no surprises. If one does everything that is proper physically, socially, and emotionally, one will live forever. Life is an interlocking network of impersonal relationships that, when broken, causes suffering and death.

"*Down deep we don't suffer*" is a third perspective. Some believe that all that is tangible and passing is not real. Suffering is derived from being too attached to what is passing. The real is always permanent. Change is not real. This "permanent" reality may be called *soul* by some, *self* by others, or *god* by still others. There are many names used to describe this permanency, but behind the names is either a claim that there is a personal individuality that never changes or there is a common, shared oneness that we all are. In either case, when we get caught up in this changing world, suffering occurs. When we get caught up in our changing individual desires, suffering occurs. Death is the deliverance from this suffering. But awareness that all of this is not real is also a way to move beyond the suffering. To realize that down deep, where the real me resides, there is no suffering, is to go beyond death to be a reality that stands still, where there is no difference between past, present, and future.

"*It all fits in somehow*" is a perspective many of us have, since it is depends on our Western culture and the classical religions that shaped its foundations. It sees time and reality not as some permanent circle, as "down deep we don't suffer," but as a vector, a line going somewhere because it has reasons to go somewhere. Our personal history takes a personal direction that results from the interplay of our freedom and our loving and working with the world we are part of. We are very much our body, our changing emotions, and our relationships. We would be nothing without these dynamic and embodied realities.

The "why" question is very important to those who approach life from this standpoint because its answer indicates to them the direction of their future and the reasonableness of their death. Suffering and death must fit into something more than oneself. This something may be titled history, God, God's will, or the kingdom of God. Again, there are many images for the plan, but behind the plan is always a suggestion that it is a personal plan. The universe and all of life is the consequence of a relationship between the individual and all living and nonliving beings, and that which supports the life and direction of this universe and life.

When one asks why we suffer, from this perspective, the expected answer is along the lines of, Why did your parent or friend hang up the phone? The expected answer is a personal answer involving love, responsibility, value, or something similar. The "why" question in the other three perspectives is an impersonal question and looks for an impersonal answer. "Why did he die?" in "It's absurd" expects a response of "There is no reason; it just doesn't makes sense." "Why did he die?" in "That's life" has an answer framed in impersonal logic such as "It's a terrible disease. Almost everyone dies because of it." "Why did he die" in "Down deep we don't suffer" is a question seldom asked. If asked, the expected reply would indicate that death has not changed the person, that suffering is always part of the life until we realize that what we think is life, is not. The "why" question may be asked in the "It all fits in somehow" perspective, but a clear and precise answer is not expected. Instead we hear themes such as "We just don't know what it's all about." "We think that what happened is bad, but we know that even from bad, good may come." Or, in a sort of ultimate personal relationship, we describe how God suffered and died and that this seems stupid yet it is believed. Notice that the general "It all fits in somehow" is accepted, but how it fits becomes lost in the mystery of the stories that are part of this approach.

Questions and Answers within Classical Spiritualities

These four answers are really spiritualities: a spirituality of the absurd, of consequence, of illusion, and of providence. We live as well as speak questions and answers. When recognized and affirmed as the plot of life, each is a spirituality that directs our lives. These four answers are also institutionalized in specific historical religious traditions.

Humans have faced suffering and death since the beginning of time. The manner in which they have responded to these two basic realities has become embodied in a number of traditions. Traditions, after all, are our patterned response to the foundational realities of life. We have traditions of eating, of sleeping, of speaking, and of suffering. This patterned response to suffering and death may be found expressed in each of the foundational human realities. Thus we have traditions of bodily care, social ritual, emotional linking, and seeking for meaning associated with death and suffering.

Because suffering and death are so all encompassing, so involved with the foundational realities of life, the traditions that are deeply involved with these questions are those we generally describe as religions and spiritualities. *Religious communities have always responded to the whole person in their dealing with death and suffering.* Some commentators in the last century, because of their philosophical orientation, suggested that religions always were concerned with the future, especially the future after this life. But if one looks at the major classical religions and their embedded spiritualities, one sees a wholistic commitment to the alleviation of the suffering of the living and to care for the dead. There is care from the perspective of physical well-being; care and concern for the sick and infirm have been so much a part of religion. Especially in the West, we have the tradition of hospitals and the vocation of doctor as evidence of a long tradition of care and cure. Every spirituality has a way of dealing with those who suffer. The one suffering should be aware of this; those who aid the sufferer should be aware of where religious help may be obtained. Google and Bing are easy sources of information for housing, food, grief, and/or other physical needs.

Every religion demands right living or right morals from its members. Right living looks toward the diminution of suffering by erasing its immediate cause. It sets the stage for a world free of the suffering caused by humans. Judaism, for instance, has given us many principles of justice and concern. The statement of God in Hosea 6:6 "what I want is love, not sacrifice" sets the prophetic theme of justice and love for all. And Nathan's statement to David, "You are the man"—that is, you are responsible and accountable to God for the suffering you cause, places the burden on the individual to relieve suffering (2 Samuel 12:7).

The Christian's obligation vis-à-vis suffering is found both in Jesus's words on the Sermon on the Mount (Matthew 5:1-12; Luke 6:20-26) and in his example in healing the blind, the lame, and the deaf. Islam's Five Pillars include a direct attack on poverty and demand the giving of alms. As the Quran says, "Did he not find you wandering and give you guidance? As for the orphan, then, do him no harm; as for the beggar, turn him not away" (Smriti xciii). For the Hindu, right living consists in specifying duties for each state of life. If lived, they decrease the suffering in the world. In essence, one should cause harm to no one. Buddhism and Hinduism find a common bond in a compassion that seeks unity with the suffering of others in order to destroy all suffering. These are some of the ways the classical forms of religion deal with the suffering that surrounds them.

Religions also offer many means of engaging the emotions surrounding suffering and death. This engagement of the emotions is found especially in the traditions of "devotion" and "mystical union." Not everyone within the various religions engages in these two traditions, but they are present in most religions.

Devotion is prayer and lifestyle committed to a significant religious figure—for example, Krishna or Jesus. Prayer is communication with this most significant religious figure. Our suffering takes on a meaning because of our relationship to this figure. At the same time, our consecration to him or her opens up patterns of endurance, compassion, and forgiveness, because we want to base our lives on the object of our devotion who has also suffered.

Mystical union is consecration brought to completion by accomplishing oneness with the ultimate in our lives. We see this in the Eastern religions, where the ultimate identity of each of us is found in the permanent (Brahman); or in the Far East, in Tao, where we can reach an inner perception of and unity with Tao. The union is with that which is beyond the here and now. In the union, there is no suffering.

The *social dimensions* of religion are many, and most of them have become enshrined in ritual: the rituals surrounding the preparation of the disposal of the body, the rituals associated with the days and/or weeks following the death, and the prayer rituals within the gathering of the community petitioning for health or comfort. Ritual action copes with suffering in many ways—for example, by enlisting the support of the religious community as in Jewish mourning practices of Shiva or in the Catholic Mass, or by placing sufferings in a positive frame of mind by putting the sufferers in contact with their ultimate concern and consequently relativizing the suffering. Some ritual actions, such as faith healing, are believed to reduce suffering itself.

Every wholistic approach must also include the human drive to understand the surrounding world. The religious traditions in response to the "why" question have developed signposts of belief over the centuries to help respond to this question. Especially in religious traditions that acknowledge a personal God (Judaism, Christianity, and Islam), there have been various attempts to understand why we suffer, why we die, and what influences our future. There are three basic responses: the instrumental, the punitive, and the redemptive.

The instrumental model of suffering is found, for instance, in the Islamic belief that suffering is an instrument of God's purposes; in Christianity, that God made Jesus perfect through suffering (Hebrews 12:3-10). In any discussion of suffering, this way of understanding the "why" of suffering comes to the fore as we tell one another that few good things are produced without pain or as we ask how we can develop into mature persons without suffering. The belief is that suffering is an instrument—sometimes sharp, sometimes blunt—of individual and communal development. A personal God uses it to bring about his goal for humanity.

Suffering considered as punishment changes the emphasis slightly yet significantly. Punishment highlights the judgmental character of a personal God. We suffer because we or others have sinned. Suffering is a way of righting the imbalance of evil over good. As Rabbi Ruba (1500 CE) said, "If a man sees that painful suffering visits him, let him examine his conduct." This approach is found in many prayer books of classic religions.

But classic religion is not alone in such an approach: The blood of many people flows in reparation for the sins of their colonial forefathers; a woman in public office is hounded from it for an offense committed in her teens; those who commit crimes against society are punished for past deeds. The model of suffering as a punishment for wrongdoing is evident to anyone who makes a child suffer because of a misdeed. It is a short step to complete the circle and ask of the sufferer what he or she has done wrong, because suffering is supposedly always linked to wrongdoing. As a Sufi saying has it: "When you suffer pain, your conscience is awakened; you are stricken with remorse and pray God to forgive your trespasses."

The belief in *suffering as redemptive* is found in many stories and songs: Someone takes upon himself or herself the sins and burdens of others so that all will be free of the consequences of sin. In this view, whenever anyone suffers so that others may live, redemption occurs. The prophets of Israel make this clear in describing the role of the Babylonian captivity in the nation's life. Isaiah summarized it when he said, "By his suffering shall my servant justify many, taking their faults on himself." John's Gospel applies this same principle to Christianity when John the Baptist claims that Jesus is the one who takes away the sins of the world (John 1:29).

Listening to the Spirituality of the Sufferer

Most spiritualities find their home in one of the classical religions. These religions originated long before our modern world. They presuppose a closeness of community and a continuity of religious membership that their contemporary adherents may not recognize. Nor are these believers aware of all the details of their religious signposts. Yet they may vaguely expect their professed religion or spirituality to provide them comfort when facing dying and death. How many times do they hear people interviewed on TV news say they have found their faith a powerful tool in the face of adversity? Hearing this in the midst of a cultural expectation that religion's role is to bring personal and communal peace, they seek some of this peace in the religion they know. They seek religion's power to reduce the pain from this prolonged, painful encounter with death. Yet many times they are ignorant of the rituals, devotions, literature, and stories that provide such relief. All the habits resultant from regular religious practice are lacking: there is no habit that kicks in automatically to deal with the numbness of the suffering that is part of the death event. In typical secular fundamentalist fashion, they seek to pick off the shelf of religion some item of belief or practice that will help them survive this ordeal. Yet they do not have the context provided by the signposts that provides that belief and practice its power to embrace the painful suffering.

A funeral ritual, for instance, may be found in most of the classical religions. Let us use the Episcopal Church as an example. Someone may have been born, baptized, and confirmed in this faith. Neither she nor her close relatives have gone to church for twenty years. The person's spouse dies at seventy-two years of age. She expects the church to provide a funeral ritual for her deceased, the priest to preach a homily, and the parish to support her in her husband's death. But she likely will not understand the ritual, because its symbols and stories are foreign to her; the homily will not be personal, because no one knows her or her husband; and the service will be attended by few because of the ages of both the deceased and his spouse. This person's professed religious membership did not reflect her true spirituality, which may have been a style or spirit quite foreign to her religion. She may actually have a spirituality more akin to Wicca.

When we listen to the suffering present in this person, who could be one of us, we gradually may become aware of the lived spirituality of the person, not the presupposed or easily articulated one from childhood as found in our example. The questions we asked above are helpful for hearing what the person is actually saying. When we ask, "What happened?" the response engages us in the other person's spirituality. The dos and don'ts of spiritual listening, plus recognition of the categories we mentioned in reviewing death and suffering, help us begin to discern that spirituality. Their present encounter with death or deep suffering may be an overwhelming challenge to that spirituality, or it may not be. Our ability to understand the story and its underlying spirituality determines the level of our involvement with that person's spirituality.

Summary

In this chapter, you were asked to look at the classical spiritualities and react positively and negatively to what they offer. Such a reaction enables you to consciously reflect on and modify your present spirituality. Appendix B provides you with the bare bones of their signposts. This chapter concentrated on their vision of self, death, and suffering.

If a spirituality is a vision and means of transcending our present life, then the way spiritualities envision that transcendence is central to the vitality of that spirituality. "Dear Diary III" will help you to clarify how you wish your life to change. What this chapter provided was an opportunity to review who was changing (you), what you would ultimately change into (the afterlife), and how to deal with the suffering you have to go through in order to change yourself. The next chapter will provide you a similar opportunity by bringing you into conversation with the marginal spiritualities.

DEAR DIARY III

SHOULD I CHOOSE A CLASSICAL HOME?

Up until this point, your dialogue partner has been yourself. You have tried to understand your spirituality by looking at your past and present. You may have entered into conversation with a friend, a spouse, or a reading group. If you have, some of what we review in the following questions has probably been discussed.

Discussion and written words are essential for dialogue. Yet they do not encompass the totality of a spirituality. A spirituality is always more than a book, no matter how sacred a book may be. People grow, love, hate, and struggle for food, water, and housing. People live, suffer, and die. Individuals never fit neatly into scientific categories. A spirituality is a way of life of a person. The written word can *never* encompass a person's life. Nevertheless, we can use the written word to build bridges toward understanding the spiritualities that surround us and to enter into dialogue with them. That is what we are doing here as we engage with some of the ideas inherent in spiritualties that have withstood the test of time while crossing national and tribal boundaries. They have existed for thousands of years, giving hope and solace to billions of people. Should your spirituality embrace one of these spiritualities?

The questions that follow are arranged first according to categories that provide a comparison between the spiritualties and then sequentially, beginning with Christianity.

In the following, who best expresses your spirituality?

Reflections….Connections…Observations

Abraham lived in the desert. He wandered with his sheep from oasis to oasis. He had two children from two different wives. He was convinced that he had an agreement (covenant) with God. He and God agreed that God would watch over him and his tribe forever, and Abraham and his tribe would direct their lives according to God's commands. Abraham's unconditional following of God's commands led him to a willingness to commit the supreme act of sacrificing one of his sons, Isaac. At the last second, God accepted Abraham's desire to follow God's will as sufficient. God stopped Abraham from killing his son. Abraham looked forward to the time when his tribe would be the largest and most prosperous in the world because he followed all of God's commands. The most famous of those who claim to be part of his tribe are called Jews, Christians, and Muslims.

Jesus was a Jew who preached that God was ready to change how people lived (Kingdom of God). He never married. Many people believed his message and began to live as he preached. Central to his preaching was that we should love God and each other, and care for those lacking the necessities of life such as food, clothing, and water. His preaching was interpreted as traitorous to both his state and his religion. He was judged and condemned to die a criminal's death—on a cross. His most devoted followers abandoned him when he went to trial. Shortly after his death, however, they became convinced that he was alive and that Jesus's new life was God's sign that God was beginning to change the world. They believed that he was the Messiah, the Christ. They continued preaching his message and living the life he preached. These first preachers were called apostles. People called those who adhered to the apostles' message about Jesus, Christians.

Muhammad is honored as God's last prophet, who received the revelation of God given by the archangel Gabriel. The Quran is the compilation of what he received. It is God's actual words. He was also a successful merchant, warrior, politician, and unifier of Arabic tribes. He was the father of seven children by twelve wives. He told us that God's will, as revealed in the Quran, must be submitted to with our whole heart and mind. Such submission will be evident in the way we pray throughout the day and obediently live our lives throughout the years. The society that follows God's revelations will be blessed by God in this life and the next. Those who are part of it will be known by their total submission to God's (Allah's) will. They are called Muslims.

Siddhartha Gautama was born a warrior, yet lived a protected life. He married and fathered one child. As he matured, he became aware of old age, suffering, and death. He realized he must defeat them to live well. His first attempt was to become a monk. He fasted, meditated, and lived an ascetical life. Being a monk did not provide him with the means to defeat these evils. One day he sat and mediated, determined to discover the means to conquer these evils. What he discovered was that everything we do is driven by desire. If we remove our desire for everything in this life, we remove suffering. If we remove desire and suffering, we realize the illusionary nature of this world, since this world is created out of our desires. We enter a new world. With such a realization, Siddhartha broke the cycle of re-incarnation. He attainted nirvana, enlightenment, perfect peace, the absence of all desire. He returned to us from nirvana to teach us how to achieve enlightenment. In doing so, he became the Buddha.

Nataputta Vardhamana, called Mahavira, also was a warrior, married, with one young daughter. He too realized there was more to life than what he had lived so far. He abandoned this wife, daughter, and warrior life and wandered naked throughout India. He wanted to live a life of self-denial and avoid attachments at all costs. He never stayed more than a day in one place. He lived a life of *ahimsa* (non-injury; nonviolence) to such an extent that he strained the water he drank through a cloth so anything living in the water would not be destroyed in his drinking. For the same purpose, he swept with a broom where he walked. Thirteen years after he began, he reached the point of complete detachment and nonviolence. His disciples recognized him as the last *tirthankara:* the last one who found a way to cross over the river of rebirth (*samsara*) to perfect peace. We know him as the founder of Jainism.

The Great Master Kung, K'ung fu-tzu (Confucius), was a teacher. After his father died, his mother sacrificed a great deal to provide him with a good education. He worked in the government bureaucracy until he was fifty. At that time he became one of the chief administrators for the local Duke of Lu. This did not work out, and he left the position. For thirteen years he wandered from state to state, teaching about how to bring about political and social reform. He returned home to the district of Lu, where he remained until he died at seventy-two. Confucius wrote many books and taught many students. It was the students who brought his teachings into everyday life. What they and Confucius taught was that we are all part of a giant, harmonic pattern of life in which each of us is to play our part. If we learn to perfect the pattern we are genetically and culturally destined to be individually and socially, we will live in harmony with self, others, and nature. Central to perfecting ourselves and the community is a life of virtue. Virtue, after all, is patterned living: a positive quality of a person that, after time and discipline, becomes part of her or his very being. The precise nature of these virtues and their implementation in everyday life became Confucianism—the foundation of Chinese culture.

> Which is your way of understanding the self (who you are)?
>
> Reflections…Connections…Observations

- I am here and now but not yet (Western).
- I am neither here nor now (Eastern, Indian).
- I am here and now, there and then (Eastern Chinese and Japanese).
- I am here and now (survival).

> Is your spirituality best described as Western, Eastern, or marginal?
>
> Reflections…Connections….Observations

- Western classical spiritualties are those spiritualities that find their origin in religions of Judaism, Christianity, and Islam.
- Eastern classical spiritualties are those that find their origins in the religions of India (Hinduism, Buddhism, Jainism, Sikhism) and of East Asia (Taoism, Shinto, and Confucianism).
- Marginal spirituality expresses the vision of those who have rejected the classical spiritualities throughout history. Today synonyms for marginal spiritualities are sects, cult, occult, esoteric, mystical, or metaphysical.

Which category best expresses your view of God? (See Glossary of Key Terms for Discussing Spiritualities…those based on views of God)

Reflections…Connections…Observations

- Monistic spirituality
- Monotheistic spirituality
- Polytheist spirituality
- Atheistic spirituality
- Agnostic spirituality

Questions	Reflections	Connections	Observations
Do you believe in God?			
Do you believe God has chosen you for a special destiny?			
Are you at ease with a spirituality that permits diverse beliefs among its followers, such as the existence and nonexistence of heaven?			
Do you follow the Ten Commandments?			

Questions	Reflections	Connections	Observations
Do you have more or less than ten commandments in your life?			
Is Judaism or parts of Judaism a viable part of your spirituality?			
Do you have a Christian Bible? Which translation is it?			
Do you think everything in the Bible should be believed?			
Do you think all the laws in the Bible should be followed?			
Are the older Christian churches attractive to you? For example, Catholic, Lutheran, Orthodox, Episcopal.			
Are the newer, Bible-based, churches attractive to you? For example, those not formally connected to any other church.			
Is it helpful for a spirituality to have one book that explains its beliefs, rituals, morals, and organizational procedures?			

Questions	Reflections	Connections	Observations
The following are some statements that have always been part of Christian creeds since the fourth century. Mark an X next to those statements you believe. • I believe in God the Father, • God the Son, • God the Holy Spirit. • I believe God created the universe. • I believe Jesus is both God and human. • I believe Jesus died. • I believe in the one holy, catholic, apostolic church. • I believe in one baptism for the forgiveness of sins. • I believe in the resurrection of the dead.			
Do you believe it is necessary to belong to an organized group to be spiritual?			
If an organized group were necessary, which of the following would be beneficial for your spirituality? • Going to a shrine when you need to petition for some personal or social need • Gathering once a week, on a special day, for worship services			

Questions	Reflections	Connections	Observations
• Gathering several times a week for fellowship and common prayer • Belonging to a group with regional (state and/or national) branches • Belonging to a group with adherents from diverse nations throughout the world			
Should a Christian spirituality include the following rituals? Answer "yes" or "no." • baptism • confirmation • Eucharist/Lord's Supper/ Communion/Mass • marriage • ordination • anointing of the sick • confessing one's sins to a person chosen to represent God and God's church			

Questions	Reflections	Connections	Observations
Is it true that to be a Christian you must affirm the following? • have a personal relationship to Jesus. • experience the fact you are saved. • be baptized. • accept the authority of the Bible. • accept the authority of those who follow in the apostles' footsteps. • be baptized in the Holy Spirit. • believe in miracles. • follow Jesus's command-ments. • frequently repeat Jesus's prayer (the Our Father/Lord's Prayer). • celebrate Christmas with fel-low Christians. • celebrate Easter with fellow Christians.			
Does your spirituality customar-ily call God • Allah • Father • God • You would never utter such a holy name.			

Questions	Reflections	Connections	Observations
Do you believe there is only one Allah (God)?			
Do you believe that God's will determines everything in your life?			
Is martyrdom an important part of your spirituality?			
Are martyrs witnesses to what God wills for us?			
Does your spirituality have any or all of the following obligations? • professing your faith • praying • fasting • giving alms • making a pilgrimage to Mecca			
Do you believe an angel will sound the end of the world and God's judgment will follow?			
Will we be judged according to whether we do certain rituals to honor God? Whether we take interest on loans? Whether we provide food, drink, and clothing for those in need?			

Questions	Reflections	Connections	Observations
Are any of the following "yoga" part of your spirituality? An important direction in you compass? • *karma* yoga (the way of action) • *bhakti* yoga (the way of devotion) • *jnana* yoga (the way of knowledge)			
Do the virtues advocated in *jnana* yoga have a place in your spirituality? • control of one's mind • control of one's senses • endurance • faith • perfect concentration, renouncing everything that is not part of dharma			
What role does love play in your spirituality?			
Do you think it is possible and/or necessary to love God or a god to deepen your spirituality?			
Is there anything your spirituality says you should not kill?			

Questions	Reflections	Connections	Observations
Does your spirituality allow you to kill anything to satisfy your desires?			
Is your soul/self always changing, as the Buddhists believe? • never born and capable of lasting forever, as many Americans claim? • dependent on the will of God for its continued existence as believers in resurrection declare? • End with your death?			
Do the Buddha's noble truths have a place in your spirituality? • All life is suffering • the cause of suffering is desire. • Stopping desire will stop suffering. • The Eightfold Path is the best way to stop desire.			

Questions	Reflections	Connections	Observations
Does your spirituality follow the Eightfold Path by being able to provide • right views? • right intention? • right speech? • right action? • right livelihood? • right effort? • right mindfulness? • right concentration?			
Is living in a monastery an ideal in your spirituality?			
Do you wish to live a compassionate life? What are your means for doing so, if you wish to?			
Is harmony among peoples necessary for the perfection of your spiritual life?			
Does your spiritual life have ways of bringing about harmony?			
Do you have anything magical in your spirituality?			

Questions	Reflections	Connections	Observations
Suffering occurs in many ways. List your most intense times of suffering. For example • Physical pain • Social alienation • Mental anguish • Death of another • Loss of a body part • Loss of a job • Loss of a spouse through divorce • Loss of a hope for a certain future • Other?			

Chapter Four

The Marginal Spiritualities

The life of those on the margins is different from those who live in the center. A description of marginal spiritualities depends on where you live your present spiritual life and its relationship to the dominant culture. Three dominant cultures influence readers of this book: medieval, modern, and liminal. Today many live in a liminal culture: a time when the meanings of words and the value of laws shift suddenly; when authority is easily challenged; and when everything is tentative because people are suspicious of ideologies, powerful people, and ancient promises.

All three cultures exist in contemporary life. The classical spiritualities described in Chapter Three are at home in the medieval cultures of the world. In those cultures, each classical spirituality is still very much a part of its calendar, laws, literature, music, customs, and values. Medieval cultures have been and are threatened by the rise of other ways of life. The word used to describe the gradual loss of centrality of place as those medieval cultures change to modern or to liminal is *secularization*. The bottom line for all the diverse definitions of secularization is that the dominant religion is losing its role in society as that society begins to adapt to a different role for science, technology, history, and all nonreligious knowledge.

Both the culture and the religion change as a consequence of modernization and liminality. The consequence of such change is that all religions and spiritualities are becoming marginalized as these cultures change. Therefore, in describing marginal spiritualities, I will first look at what is happening to the classical spiritualities as they exist in contemporary cultures and then I will look at those spiritualties that were considered marginal when the classical ones dominated the culture.

Four Centers and Their Margins

A skeletal summary of Western culture provides us with four types of spirituality: survival, medieval, modern, and liminal

Survival/indigenous spirituality. Here, the promise of a perfected present in the future is promoted by the myths and rituals engaged in by individuals and community. Any imperfections of the present are overcome by using the rituals provided by tradition. In doing so, the necessary food, marriage arrangements, secure personal interactions, and healthy life are enabled. Those on the margins are other peoples (tribes) who do not share the ritual, traditions, and family bonds of the tribe.

Medieval spirituality in the West was founded on the vision and hierarchical nature of Roman Catholicism between 900 CE and 1500 CE A life with God is promised and promoted by the proper use of sacraments and encouragement of habits that avoid the seven deadly sins of lust, gluttony, greed, sloth, envy, anger, and pride and encouraging the virtues opposite to them of chastity, temperance, charity (generosity), diligence (hard work), patience, kindness (compassion), and humility. Medieval theology offered a critique of both church and government using the tools of reason, especially logic, inherited from the ancient Greeks and Romans. From 1100 CE, witches, Jews, and pagans of all sorts were viewed as threats to the dominant culture.

Modern spirituality promises a future world made perfect through the use of the sciences and their derivatives. Many modern spiritualities are characterized by a secular fundamentalist outlook with certitude and fellowship derived from scientific facts and theories based on the hard and soft sciences. Gradually, most forms of Christianity along with other religions were considered marginal. Anything that was clearly irrational was seen as a threat to society; thus all paranormal claims were distrusted and ways of life that accepted these claims were powerless in modern society.

Liminal spiritualities are embedded with uncertainty, tentativeness, and a suspicion of all ideologies and communities that demand total commitment over a prolonged period. The signposts of the past that embedded the ancient religious visions, promises, and means of achieving them are experienced as unproductive in resolving present challenges. Yet hope is the energizing force that shapes, and reshapes their signposts. Such hope easily attaches itself to charismatic personalities who offer a salve to present pain by energizing a hope for tomorrow obtained with little personal effort. Reason and the rule of scientific and expert knowledge are distrusted in the general populace that lives off their fruits. There is no center in this liminal age. Everyone inhabits the niche reflected in their social network. The result is a great deal of networking without any sharing equivalent to the necessary spiritual signposts for a spiritual life. This networking may change, however, as the socialization process converts it into a new type of community.

A more complete description of the last three of these cultures may be found in appendix A, "Three Foundational Cultures." The question you must answer is which of these cultures best supports your envisioned spirituality. To help you do that, I will first present secular fundamentalism as a dominant perspective in our current culture and then offer an interpretation of what is happening to the classical spiritualities. There is little doubt that the classical spiritualities reflect in both a positive and negative fashion the liminal age in which they now exist. There is no unity within or between any of the classical spiritualities, and each classical spirituality is composed of diverse interpretations of its way of life. Some of those interpretations are an embodiment of a dominant worldview called secular fundamentalism. Some are a rejection of that worldview. Others are an attempt to move beyond such an influential perspective as secular fundamentalism.

Secular Fundamentalism: Ideas Clearly Stated and Understood Will Result in a Perfect Society

Secular fundamentalism, referred to in the following as fundamentalism, is a worldview in which all of life and its experiences are interpreted literally rather than symbolically and uniformly rather than pluralistically. It is a way of seeing and interpreting our world that demands that those significant words that are expressive of meaning and belonging be identical from context to context. It is also a movement of those seeking companionship among those of like mind in such a way that the world is cast in a we-them dichotomy. As both a worldview and a movement, its adherents accept certain conceptual signposts and normative attitudes as marks of the good and truthful person. This set of experiences, conceptual signposts, and normative attitudes make up the hermeneutical circle of fundamentalism. They are connected to each other so that one cannot exist without the other.

Several attitudes constitute the fundamentalist experience. First is a realization of a strong, easily distinguishable difference between those who are good and speak the truth and those who are not good and do not speak the truth. There is uneasiness, sometimes bordering on anger, when some people describe themselves as sincere but really are not. These nominally sincere people may lack some of the conceptual signposts and/or the attitudes necessary to be a good person. Whatever it is that these other people lack, the fundamentalist realizes that he or she does have these concepts and experiences while others do not. The reason the fundamentalist can claim such knowledge is because he or she has had those unique experiences that are the foundation of being good and truthful. In the fundamentalist world, one does not have to investigate, have oaths or creeds, or have long discussions. One senses quickly when one is in the presence of a truly sincere person, because that person has shared some of the same experiences. One becomes accustomed to how it feels to be in the nominally good and truthful person's presence, and thus one learns to sense when a person is good and truthful and when not.

Second, the fundamentalist has an optimistic outlook that is not a mental operation but a deeply felt experience. Such an outlook can best be described as a feeling of confidence that if the world takes the direction envisioned by the truly good and truthful people, it will be the best possible world. The fundamentalist is optimistic that this world will come about if everyone has confidence and works hard to do what is necessary for this new world to come.

Third, the fundamentalist is aware of a source of special energy, vitality, and dynamism resultant from this confidence. Sometimes a fundamentalist is able to do things because of this confidence that he or she would never otherwise do. But confident in her abilities and optimistic of the outcome, she is able to move to new heights of goodness and truth as a result of being at one with the true purpose of the universe.

Fourths, truth is experienced. It is felt, touched, and discovered. Such empirical truth is found in the written and spoken word. These words give security and provide a constant and clear authority in personal as well as communal life.

Fifth, one expresses these feelings in inner thoughts of gratitude for being good and for knowing the truth—hoping beyond hope that life will be good. In the midst of such inner thoughts, the fundamentalist feels energized in such a way that he can do no wrong because he is associated with those who are good and possess the truth.

These feelings result in easily identifiable words, phrases, and statements that establish a conceptual framework for experiences. Slogans, propaganda statements, advertising jingles, and repeated phrases and value statements are the ordinary ways in which these verbalizations are expressed. These words and phrases are a summary of the way the fundamentalist sees the world. They are also a ritual incantation that expresses the fact that one has had the experience and shares the common outlook to which these words witness. Agreeing on such a common way of expressing oneself on the fundamentals, the fundamentalist is freed to do and think whatever she may wish. The ideas expressed are clearly demonstrated and agreed on by all. It is upon these ideas, expressed in easily understood words, that a perfect society can be built.

Pluralism, uncertainty, and competition for the power to direct cultural forces are inherent to a liminal culture. Secular fundamentalism, as a process, provides a way to diminish uncertainty, provide unity, and give a clear direction to the symbols that compose a culture. It is a strong force in business, politics, and religion. It is one of the stronger reactions to modern and liminal cultures and is included below under the traditionalist response to cultural change.

Classic Spiritualities in a Liminal Culture

The classic religions and their spiritualities have responded in three ways to our contemporary situation. We will call these responses traditionalist, contemporalist, and co-temporalist. First, the *traditionalists* rejected all that threatened them and sought to return to what they described as the tradition. Some Christians, for example, demanded that Christian churches return to the fundamentals as reflected in their Bible, while others sought to embody the ideals and dress of medieval times. Second, the *contemporalists* countered the threats of modernity by absorbing them whole into their religious/spiritual life while rejecting what no longer fit in their present life. For example, their present life was best lived in accord with social and physical sciences rather than by following ancient kosher laws. The Unitarian-Universalist movement is an example of this response. Third, the *co-temporalists* sought to understand the basic nature of the modern and its expressions, so they might include them in their present life without destroying their former spiritual identity. Many deeply spiritual people, as a consequence, felt that both the truths of their classical spirituality and the truths of the sciences both had a great deal to contribute to their lives. Thus both the sciences and their spirituality were re-examined to discover the necessary truths for contemporary living.

These three divisions, with the titles I have given them, are clearly seen within Judaism as the Orthodox (traditionalists), Conservative (co-temporalists), and Reform (contemporalist) movements. The Orthodox retain all the ancient *mitzvoth*, or laws, as well as celebrate the Sabbath and High Holidays in ancient Hebrew. The Conservatives retain all mitzvoth still found viable in this modern world and have a mixture of ancient Hebrew and English in worship. The Reform has services on Sunday, in English, and sporadically keep kosher. People within each classical spirituality have responded in one of these three ways to the challenge of how to understand, live, and communicate their spirituality to others in our contemporary world.

I cannot possibly describe in detail the diversity found among the classical religions. The select bibliography and websites in the Resources at the end of the book provide you with ways to follow up an interest you may have.

The Traditionalists

The traditionalists look to imitation of the past as the promise to transcend present evils and the deep uncertainty found in the present spiritual signposts. Many times this takes the form of a literal imitation of exactly what was believed and done in the past. If the present imitates the past and is seen as good, the future in this or another world will be better. Many examples are found in the diverse classical spiritualities.

The most evident one in US culture is Christian fundamentalism. In the spirit of secular fundamentalism, it looks to an inerrant and God-inspired Bible as the proclaimer of right thought and correct living. "Conversation" and "revival" are the foundational rituals wherein the participants experience Jesus's concern for them, their faults, their errors, and their sins. This concern is experienced in the intensity of Jesus's forgiveness and their salvation. Saved from the fires of hell, they join with others who are saved. With the Bible in hand, they possess the compass for their spiritual life. The foundational ideas, or beliefs, are the virgin birth of Christ; the inspiration of the Bible by the Holy Spirit and the inerrancy of Scripture as a result of this inspiration; Christ's death was the atonement for sin; the bodily resurrection of Christ; and the historical reality of Christ's miracles.

Pentecostal and charismatic spirituality is the fastest growing branch of Christianity. It looks to the experience of the apostles at Pentecost as the foundational experience for contemporary living. Pentecostal and charismatic spirituality are characterized by a deeply felt experience of the Holy Spirit's presence, called Spirit baptism, and the signs that accompany this experience, especially talking in tongues. The terms *Pentecostal* and *charismatic* are used to distinguish between those having this foundational experience and their institutional embodiments. "Pentecostals" are usually found in Bible-based, evangelical, and fundamentalist Protestant churches. Purely fundamentalist churches usually reject the Pentecostal assertion that the spiritual gifts present among early Christians are present today. "Charismatics" are usually found in churches that are tradition based, such as Roman Catholicism, Anglicanism, and Lutheranism.

Christian identity groups and militias are spiritualities that attract those with a deep love of a past dominated by male, white Americans. They combine selected Bible quotes with a nostalgic view of American history before the Civil War to promise a new world of social dominance for like-minded individuals. Their means for bringing this new word into existence is violent revolution when necessary or intimidation when possible.

Every classical spirituality has large elements of its population that seek future advancement through reproducing past histories of dominance and imagined perfect spiritual living. Many of those seeking such a future do so through the lens of secular fundamentalism. Islam is a special case of such seeking, because it is the second largest religion in the world, and Arabic Muslims are in control of great oil reserves. All of Islam may be seen as interpreting the Quran in a literal and legalistic manner. The implementation of sharia law among Sunni and Shia Muslims is both very logical and extremely dependent on past interpretations.

The two best national examples of such traditionalism and fundamentalism are Iran and Saudi Arabia. Here God's will is easily translated into the laws that rule everyday commerce and life. If such an approach to living a spiritual life is attractive to you, it is best that you go live there before making any decisions. The more mystical approach to Islam is Sufism. Where one lives is not a necessary condition for coming into contact with God (Allah) when the ancient Sufi methods are employed. These are best learned from a Sufi spiritual master.

The Contemporalists

Contemporalists accept almost carte blanche the dominant perspective of the surrounding culture. Every classical spirituality has been contemporalist in the past, since it has been a national religion. Today many contemporalists look to the sciences and the scientific method as the norm for life. While on the margins in a liminal culture, science-contemporalists have, and still do in some circles, enjoy the affirmation of the majority. Remember that, in this case, science includes psychology, sociology, and anthropology.

I would like to remind you that most people know very little about religion and science. As a consequence, when they develop a spirituality that they call scientific or adapt signposts they think are religious, they are usually doing so with little reference to what professionals in those fields think or practice. When an individual or group of people adapts to the modern, therefore, there is a great deal of room for the imagination in their spirituality. Here are three examples of contemporalist spiritualities.

The Self-Help Movements: Religious Science and the Twelve Steps

Particular self-help publications, communities, and websites promise and promote methods to satiate a person's desire to change herself and transcend the here and now of life for another one. Instead of the signposts of the classical religions, the self-help movement offers signposts that replace the supernatural with mental powers demonstrated, they say, by science. Émile Coué de Châtaigneraie (1857–1926) summarized it well with his suggested phrase for improving your life: "Every day, in every way, I'm getting better and better." The power of the magical repetition of such phrases is believed to empower the mind to create your present and future.

Belief in one's self and the power of one's mind is caught up in the double-bind situation. This is found in the idea that if you wish (pray) for something with strength, optimism, and perseverance, it will come true; if it does not happen, it is because you wished (prayed) with a weak, pessimistic, and tenuous attitude. Norman Vincent Peale (1898–1993), in his *The Power of Positive Thinking,* popularized this spirituality among many Americans. Many of his famous quotes still resound from pulpits and pundits across the continent: Believe it is possible to solve your problem and it will be solved. Tremendous things happen to the believer. So believe the answer will come. It will. When life hands you a lemon, make lemonade.

Twelve-Step spiritualities imitate the twelve step program of Alcoholics Anonymous with slight adjustments, depending on the type of addiction that is their concern. Here is a partial list of these imitators: Celebrate Recovery, Gamblers Anonymous, Sexual Compulsives, Pills Anonymous, Marijuana Anonymous, Crystal Meth Anonymous, Debtors Anonymous, Overeaters Anonymous, Co-Dependents Anonymous, Cocaine Anonymous, Narcotics Anonymous, Adult Children of Alcoholics, SOS (Secular Organizations for Sobriety), Cocaine Anonymous, and Overeaters Anonymous.

The Isms: Nationalism and Scientism

Every spirituality, whether shaped from personal concerns and transcendent desires or accepted from surrounding choices, has a narrative. The science fiction stories of Ron Hubbard, retold within the Church of Scientology, provide Scientologists with such a narrative about we Thetans and our fall and the necessary means to return to where we came from. A narrative is the pair of glasses through which we read the past and present, and choose a possible future. The narrative places the signposts on the road to transcendence and focuses our attention on how to walk that road, what may prevent us from taking that walk, and where the road leads.

Our socialization process includes bits and pieces of a narrative (we don't have school on Presidents' Day), a central part of the story (Christmas celebrates Jesus's birth), or the entire narrative (the film *Little Buddha*). We hear many stories. Some of these stories become part of our spirituality. Joseph Campbell suggests that such stories perform four functions: *cosmological*, they explain how the whole universe works for and against us; *sociological*, they affirm the necessity of keeping communal rules and customs so they work in our favor; *pedagogical*, they teach us how to act in order to live well; *mystical*, in the telling of the story there is the constant opportunity for a deep spiritual/sacred experience. He, as many others do, calls these profound and influential stories "myths." To those outside the myth-telling community, these stories are false and misleading; to those of the community, they are sacred and never to be contradicted.[20]

One "ism" that has produced much death and exhilaration is *nationalism*. The nation and its expressions become the means through which one finds transcendence. Its founding documents, rituals, polity, and heroic citizens become the object of its adherents' total obedience, loyalty, and dedication. The nation-narrative is usually composed of diverse themes brought together by an overarching need of the individual or group. In the case of the United States, this is usually seen as accepting as its sacred scriptures the Constitution and the Gettysburg Address; rituals such as Fourth of July, Thanksgiving, and Christmas; moral necessities such as hard work and equality; polity such as democracy; values such as capitalism, competition, freedom, and individualism. Its enemies are usually depicted as socialism, communism, and modern liberalism.[21]

The spirituality of scientism embraces only those signposts that express scientific facts: beliefs coincide with and are demonstrated by the scientific method and its results. The rituals and moral imperatives encourage healthy human development and fit within the constructs of the social sciences. You associate with those who think like you do and find it exhilarating to hear new ideas and use new technologies

Becoming a Liminal Spirituality

Contemporary liminal spiritualities abound. Many are found in the next section dealing with marginal spiritualities that have gained acceptance, though not adherence, among many in that culture. Wicca and witchcraft are examples of such spiritualities that have adapted to the spirit of liminality. Some of the modern spiritualities, in their attempt to remain relevant to the majority of people, gradually begin to accept the uncertainty, tentativeness, and suspicion present in contemporary liminality. Consequently, there is a tension between how they adapted to the modernity of the past and the challenge of adapting to the liminality of the present. If a spirituality is truly, a contemporalist one, then it will naturally seek to be liminal in liminal times and modern in modern times. A good example of this is the Unitarian Universalist Association, which is a current wave of spirituality with deep roots in past Christian cultures. These seven principles of Unitarian Universalist congregations provide a sense of this spirituality:

- the inherent worth and dignity of every person;
- justice, equity, and compassion in human relations;
- acceptance of one another and encouragement to spiritual growth in our congregations;
- a free and responsible search for truth and meaning;
- the right of conscience and the use of the democratic process within our congregations and in society at large;

- the goal of world community with peace, liberty, and justice for all; and
- respect for the interdependent web of all existence, of which we are a part. [22]

Co-temporalist (Traditioning) Spiritualities

Certainly the materials that encompass the classics change: the paper on which their holy scriptures is written; the buildings within which worship is celebrated; the words that Buddha, Jesus, or Abraham first spoke; the clothes people wear; and the language used to express the thoughts of the founders. Contemporary historical methods demonstrate that every religion and spirituality has changed significantly over the centuries in each of its signposts. So, what is there about the classical spiritualities—or any spirituality for that matter—that is ageless? Shouldn't we all just totally change our spirituality depending on our feelings and culture and be contemporalists? Is there really something about the classics that continues over the millennia, enabling each of them to fulfill the promise of the life they promote today, beyond new feelings and new culture?

The *traditionalist* approach claims that the first articulation of their signposts do not and should not change: change the material expression of their way of life, and you change that expression. Destroying those original words, beliefs, rituals, moral demands, and ways to associate with those inside and outside the spirituality is to destroy something that has given a spiritual life to millions. So, if the Quran is written in Arabic, no other language is capable of expressing God's word.

The *contemporalists* say the opposite. If you demand everything remain the same as it was in the beginning, you have changed it without acknowledging it. When you said God was Father in the past, it meant God was the source of everything, as their understanding of procreation told them. Today the Father does only part of the procreative job. The term today means something different than previously. If women were not leaders at the beginning of your religion in 2000 BCE, and you do not allow them to be so today, you are discriminating against women. When the previous manner of expressing the beliefs, rituals, morals, and communal life age or change, so does the spirituality. After all, if you change everything about you—body, past, ideas, actions, and associates—what is there to identify you as "you"? The spirituality that people live today is nothing like it was at its origins; history demonstrates nothing is the same. So, the contemporalists say, Admit it. Abandon it. Develop something new that is more healthily lived in today's culture.

The *co-temporalists* accept the paradox of change and not change, accept the paradoxes we reviewed in Chapter Two, especially, "I am an immortal who dies," understanding immortality as no-change. They sense that out of the tension of the paradox comes the renewed vigor of a spirituality seeking its identity and meaning for contemporary life. They point to the history of how each spirituality is an example of what has happened over the ages and how there is deep and significant change, yet something is the same about it. There is some pattern that continues that is not necessarily attached to the material realities of the tradition and that is independent of changing language and culture. It is not tradition that is central to a classical spirituality but traditioning—the enlivening pattern of the past in the present that is continually providing a deep spirituality for those who will live it in the future. It is this approach to spirituality I would like to focus on.

There are two ways of trying to understand how to go about developing healthy change: the mechanistic and the organic. The *mechanistic* seeks to discover the essential, abstract core of the spirituality in as objective a manner as possible. This core, then, is used as the norm of all present and future development of a spirituality. In the process the spirituality is reduced to its essential ideas, and from these one builds a healthy spiritual life——just as a person has an idea of a chair and builds a chair. So, for example, Christianity is "essentially" doing good to one's neighbor or is "essentially" faith in Jesus as Savior or, as in the early Christian church, it is where bishops, Bible, and creed are found. All else is relative.

The *organic* approach recognizes the mystery of the spiritual life in its wholeness; realizes that life is not an abstraction; accepts the fact that organisms develop after birth (for example, an apple seed does not look like an apple tree); commits to a life of liminality; and continually looks at the present to see what is alive from the past to enliven the present and the future. One looks to the past not with a nostalgic sense of returning to the past as past, but with a transcendent hope in the present for the past's evolution to a healthy future. A person does not know whether she is successful until after she has lived it. Only after living the spirituality over a prolonged period does she sense that she is in the tradition and has traditioned appropriately. We cannot be told what we experience is authentic to the religion or spirituality; we must experience it as such.

When we review the classic spiritualities, we see that there were different types of each of them. We could talk about Orthodox Christians, Catholic Christians, Pentecostal Christians; about Sunni and Shia Muslims; Theravada, Mahayana, and Vajrayana Buddhists; and so on for Judaism, Taoism, Confucianism, and Shinto. The co-temporalist thread throughout these religions reflects a number of characteristics: they retain many of their original expressions of the signposts; they contain remnants of the diverse ages within which they existed and co-temporalized in; they have an attitude of adaptation as a means of solving contemporary issues; they have a deep commitment to continuing their spiritual traditions by making them alive in the contemporary age; they find truth, beauty, and goodness both in their tradition and their culture.

Thus, for example, the mainline Christian churches in the United States during the nineteenth and twentieth centuries accepted modern methods for interpreting ancient literature and applied these methods to the Bible; rejected the ways capitalism denigrated workers and their families by preaching and applying the social gospel; rethought Christian belief in the light of the physical sciences through looking for other ways of describing miracles, the existence of heaven, the nature of the soul, and evolution; accepted the core principles of psychology in its pastoral counseling and conclusive scientific evidence.

Every classical spirituality has had to deal with a new culture. Examples from the past abound. Pictures and statues of Jesus and Buddha reflect diverse cultures that each religion has adapted to and developed within over the centuries. The diverse types of architecture of the church, the mosque, the Shinto temple reflect the religion's entry into the different cultures. Many times the actual place where the structure is built reflects the sacredness of the place—for example, a church or mosque is built on the previous church or mosque, which itself was built on a previous holy site. Christmas is a typical example of such development, as no one knows when Jesus was born. December 25 originally was a day for Romans to celebrate their sun god. Ideas such as "God" and the Christian creed are in constant development, from the Jewish *Yahweh* through the Greek *Theos* to contemporary times, when the theologian Paul Tillich called God "the Ground of Being."

As those living these diverse religions came into a culture, they had to act in a co-temporal manner. As those who came from that culture accepted the "new" religion, they acted in a co-temporal manner. Otherwise, they would have abandoned the new culture they were becoming part of. Those new to the culture learned the language, the central ideas, and the ways of acting and celebrating. The local people, who accepted the religion/spirituality as their own, chose words, ideas, and ways of acting and celebrating that they felt best expressed this new religion—now theirs. Both those old to the religion and those new to the religion took the risk of making the religion alive to their present culture.

That risk is called hope, and the confidence that this spirituality could live in any culture is called faith. If indeed the spirituality is a classic and is meant for all cultures, then it must be co-temporal to be alive for these people in these times. Otherwise, it has an appeal only to a small group of people and must abandon its mission of being a way of life for all. The result today is religions and spiritualties that have existed over the centuries. The challenge today for the classical spiritualities is to acknowledge that change happens to all of us—and that spiritual change happens to all of us. All organisms must change or die.

The co-temporal existence of the past is easily forgotten by those who know it as "the tradition." Such a spirituality is "just the way things are" to each generation. Thus each generation lives the spirituality as if it never had a history and was timeless. An historical consciousness tells us otherwise. Each spirituality today is faced with the quandary of what to do to sustain its identity. Some say, in a fundamentalist fashion, that everything must remain the same; sameness is identity. Some say it's impossible to sustain a single identity in a liminal age; sameness does not exist. Others say that only by traditioning the past into the present will the identity be sustained.

For those who accept the co-temporal as being necessary to developing a spirituality, these same co-temporal impulses are usually found in the cities and suburbs where they live. There will be found those risking the new, while holding on to the old; seeing the sources of transcendence present within the signposts in a new way and embracing new sources never before recognized. This risk means uncertainty—something the other two options do not offer. The communities will reflect the characteristics I have already provided.

Every religion and spirituality tends to ossification and, consequently, restriction of where the transcendent may become manifest. They forget that their founders discovered another way of seeing life other than the religion they were brought up in. In their profound experience of transcendence and its associated feelings, they sometimes do not realize that other co-religionists in their own generation or the next generations have neither the experience nor the expectations they have in their ways of life. Co-temporalists would suggest that in what many authorities in the classical religions call secular or scientific is found the seeds of the future of religion and the spiritualities that enliven us.

Always on the Margin: Themes and Paradigms

A marginal spirituality is one in which people live alongside of, in opposition to, or separate from the majority religious culture. Those of the majority religions often look at those on the margins with fear, curiosity, and abhorrence: with fear because they do not understand the marginal; curiosity because the unknown always tempts them to promised pleasures and forbidden knowledge; abhorrence because their difference is so great that it is a deep threat to their way of life.

Throughout history, the marginal spiritualities have been known as sects, cults, the occult, the esoteric, the mystical, or the metaphysical. For the classical Western religions, the marginal were seen as satanic, witches, pagans, idol worshipers, lost souls, or heathens. The Eastern classical religions usually described those adhering to marginal spiritualities as ignorant, worshipers of powerless gods, uncivilized, or unenlightened. Of course, the modern majority sees all religious ways of life as superstitious, unscientific, mere opinion, and uneducated. In liminal times, such as the present, all spiritualities are equal among a populace that does not understand science, religion, or spirituality and that is uncertain about most everything.

Themes among Contemporary Marginal Spiritualities

To aid you in your search for a spirituality, I have summarized the major themes of those spiritualities that are marginal to the classical spiritualities of the past and the present. We have already seen these themes in Chapter One. Here they are cast in the language of our liminal culture. In addition, I have provided the major paradigms, or models, that encompass present marginal offerings outside the classical spiritualties. I have accompanied these paradigms with their most notable examples. For a more detailed description of the spiritualities that are used as examples, there are references in the bibliography; they also may be found in my *Spiritualities: Past, Present, and Future.*

Consciousness, witness, verbalization. A marginal spirituality must, by its very nature, be ready to speak up for itself in the face of the majority, thus highlighting the necessity of consciousness, witness, and verbalization. Words, written and spoken, form the principal means of telling others about the spirituality. Community and ritual, while always present, are given subordinate positions in spiritualities that feel they need to tell others about themselves. The "telling" is always in the form of how the spirituality benefits the practitioner and provides that practitioner with means of advancement both personal and social

Quick life change. The self-help movements have influenced these spiritualties by promising near instantaneous change in one's personal life. Just as the majority of religions do not see witness as a necessary requirement for their spiritualities, most do not seek a quick life change as a necessary guarantee to the transformative power of the religion. Slow, continual growth and depth in the religious way of life is usually seen as a marker of that transformative power.

Centrality of the individual person. If it doesn't help you, it is not for you. Reflecting the extreme individualism of contemporary life, these spiritualties are focused on the individual person, not on the community. This individualism is cast in a pragmatic mode with the spirituality providing a direct stimulus to the individual's well-being.

Distrust of institutions is combined with a demand for simple solutions to any problem or conflict. Since the individual is at the center of the spirituality, the signpost of community and its possible expression in institutional demands is rejected as peripheral to the spiritual quest. The "we" is always seen as a threat to "me." The necessary freedom to do as I please, as long as it does not hurt others, is understood to be foundational to all social living.

Conscious promotion of spiritual basics (survival spirituality). Spiritual basics are what I have called the spirituality of survival. These basics consist of signposts that provide a means of entering into, coping with, and coming out of transformative events that challenge all of us: birth, suffering, marriage, death, job, personal relationships, and, what we call today, self-image. Magic ritual, a signpost essential to survival spirituality, provides that evidence to those living survival spirituality. The classic religions satisfied these basic spiritual needs throughout the centuries but for one reason or another (perhaps the influence of modernity), they do not emphasize them today.

New revelations. The old is never just old among marginal spiritualities. It is always "newly discovered." The newly discovered, but many times acknowledged in the spirituality as ancient, are usually described as being almost destroyed by the institutional religion of the time, or as ancient manuscripts or artifacts dug up in a field, ancient monastery, or library of some sort. But the old is new again because it offers a new spirituality to those bored by, offended by, or dismissive of the contemporary dominant spiritualities.

Expert spiritual guides open the doors of spiritual mysteries. All are equal in the spiritual quest, but some are more equal than others. All of these marginal spiritualities trace their origins to a spiritual master: someone who has had a special revelation of transcendental reality. The master's revelation is to be transmitted to all. Belief in this revelation marks both the master and those who follow her or him as special in knowledge and unique in the spiritual quest.

Shopping for a spirituality that fits one's transcendent desires, hopes, and expectations is a natural expression of life in a consumer society. When people begin to say they chose a religion and that they prefer this one rather than that one, we have entered a new religious and spiritual era.[23]

Religions must in some way become competitive with each other when they depend on individuals for their daily sustenance. Such competitiveness, built on individual preference, has a profound effect on the diversity of marginal spiritualities that enter into the market. It becomes a market in which the god depends on the people's choice rather than God choosing a people.

Paradigms of the Marginal Spiritualties: Nature, Spirit, Mind, Totally Different, and Action.

A paradigm is a comprehensive way of seeing and acting in our social and ideational world. Each paradigm provides us with a way of acting differently from the majority in our culture. Our way of thinking and acting is both a commentary on the majority culture as well as an advocacy for another way of thinking and acting. In addition to the themes mentioned above, the following paradigms have a deep effect on current marginal spiritualties.

Nature

Adherents to these spiritualities base their signposts on what the senses perceive and physics describes as "natural." Earth, air, fire, and water are understood to be the foundations of our life. These foundations interact and produce power or energy to change our surrounding world as the proper words and actions are performed to focus these energies for the celebrants' purposes. The purpose may be good (for example, heal my child) or evil (for example, destroy my neighbor's garden). Wiccan spirituality along with some forms of Satanism set their signposts in this "natural" world. The Western Kabbalah tradition, as well as many interpretations of Zohar, also brings into play the nature paradigm.

Spirit

The "spirit" signposts are revelatory beacons exposing us to particular beings that inhabit a parallel universe to our own. The beings are said to be "spirits" in imitation of the enlivening spirit found in every human being. Those who live in this parallel universe are not ordinarily accessible by our senses or able to be enlisted to act in our universe. The diverse spiritualities adhering to this paradigm have developed the means through which these spirits are able to be seen and harnessed to act in accord with the wishes of a priest, priestess, or shaman. This parallel universe is inhabited by both good and evil spirits (that is, those of benefit to human and those destructive of humans). Witches, Vodoun (Voodoo), Santeria, Shamans, Cabbalists (Kabbalahists), and some types of Gnostics adhere to the paradigm. Angels and devils in the monotheistic religions also may fit into this paradigm.

Mind

While usually placing the "mind" in the brain, this paradigm affirms the mind as independent of the brain and capable of controlling all material reality—including the human body. Certainly the Gnostics would see the mind (understood as spirit) as an independent controlling agency. Other marginal spiritualities using this paradigm are New Thought and the Power of Positive Thinking.

Totally Different

This paradigm begins with a conscious effort to look outside your surrounding culture to discover an ancient spirituality capable of providing you with all the benefits of your culture while living separate from it. Many times this is a conscious rejection of the dress, thought, and action of the majority. Consequently people look to Buddhist, Hindu, Jainist, or other centers in the United States with a desire to become as much a part of not only the spirituality represented there but the entire lifestyle as well. Thus you would eat, drink, dress, and sleep as the monks or nuns do at a Buddhist Center. Colonel Henry Still Olcott (1832–1907), a founder of Theosophy, became so much identified with Buddhism that some Buddhists in South East Asia considered him a Bodhisattva. Theosophy would be such a spirituality because it reformulated many Eastern religious themes for Western audiences. Some who practice yoga, transcendental meditation, and chanting take on the environment of the homeland to live their adopted spirituality in a deeper fashion.

The same might be said of those who reject the surrounding Western spiritualities for those of the Native Americans. On the one hand, many people look at these spiritualities in the light of "mind" or "nature" as mentioned above. There are some, however, who would return to nature with the idea of following the lifestyle of one of the ancient aboriginal tribes. It should be mentioned that discovering the authentic past lifestyles of an ancient aboriginal tribe is extremely difficult, since most were oral cultures; there are no written materials telling us what happened in their distant past.

Action

Our current culture is seen by many as materialistic, paternalistic, consumerist, militaristic, individualistic, environmentally polluted, and overly dependent on consistent growth. Out of this vision of our contemporary culture, those following this spirituality see a need for change in both self and society. This paradigm primarily emphasizes action over ideology and communal need over individual aggrandizement. It is co-temporalist in nature, since it is always searching for the signposts necessary to transform the present into a peaceful society of equals in a world capable of providing everyone with the minimum of food, housing, clean air, water, and health care for a just society.

Numerous movements hold to the basic paradigm of necessary action to stop present degradation as described above. Doctors Without Borders, Greenpeace, Occupy, and diverse women's movements are a few examples. The Catholic Worker movement is an example of those who live in a poor area, seeking to live a simple life and aid those in need. There are so many others that may be found in your area if you are interested in doing something that requires action.

Many spiritualties we have reviewed in this book diagnose our present culture in the same way. Some say no to that culture by seeking to return to the past to discover their future. Some say no by helping you control your thoughts and feelings so you will not be affected by this diagnosis. Some demand that you move to deserted areas of our globe to find solace away from all the degradation. Action spirituality says yes to the people who surround you and differ radically from you. It says, "Do something about the destructive attitudes and actions." It promises and promotes that, in doing something you will experience transcendence and create a world transcendent from the destructive one that has given you birth and promises uncertainty and fear for the future. It is a liminal spirituality because it is uncertain of current power structures and the language, art, and literature that support your present life. It is co-temporal because it seeks to take the best of the past and tradition it to the future. It is hopeful because it promises hope in the actions to create a just world.

Summary

In our liminal world, the classic spiritualities are challenged by remnants of the modern and the present distrust of authoritarian certitudes. They are also challenged by the fact that many transcendent experiences are found outside the traditional religions that claim to be the sole providers of authentic spiritual experiences.

Those enlivened by the energizing power of the classical spiritualities react to the challenges of cultural liminality and marginal advancement in three ways: (1) by rejecting all that threatens them and attempting to return to what is described as tradition; (2) by accepting all that is demonstrably true by science and/or experience and rejecting everything in their spirituality that is not demonstrable by scientific methods; (3) by responding slowly to these challenges and slowly testing their spirituality by revisiting its history in the light of present challenges, experience, and data offered by the sciences. They envision their spiritual path as enlivened by manifesting the truths of the past in the language of the present.

These responses of the classical spiritualities are no guarantee of future prominence. There are many challenges to their past dominance in the culture. The self-help movements, for example, provide effective means of transcendence for many in our society. Nationalism and scientism provide coherent narratives as powerful to many contemporary people as those found in the scriptures and traditions of the classical spiritualities. The themes and paradigms of the marginal spiritualties are easily found among contemporary forms of the classical spiritualties. Their discovery there challenges the identity of the present classics with the past ones.

The question for you is, "What are the themes and paradigms within your spirituality, and are these enlivening and authentic to who you are and wish to be?"

DEAR DIARY IV

SHOULD I CHOOSE A HOME DIFFERENT FROM THE MAJORITY?

You probably have a general outline of your spirituality by now. What you will be doing in this "Dear Diary" is comparing it with ways of thinking and living that may seem strange to you. But, then again, maybe they do not seem strange. Some of the spiritualities we talked about in Chapter Four may be what you identify spirituality with.

In a liminal culture, it is difficult to say what is on the margin and what is part of the mainstream. In the long run, it makes no difference because the focus of "Dear Diary" is on you and your choices. You learn just as much about your spirituality when you are able to say no to certain ideas and practices and yes to others. You have certainly said that about some of the classical spiritualities; now we look at those considered marginal in the past and, in many quarters, in the present. I will offer you choices based on what is written in Chapter Four as well as introduce elaborations on what is written there.

Questions	Reflections	Connections	Observations
Does any particular religion influence the making of national, state, and local laws?			
Do you want religion to have more or less influence on your culture?			

Questions	Reflections	Connections	Observations
Would your spirituality lead you to engage your time and energy so it had more influence?			
Using the material in Chapter Four and appendix A, respond to the following. Which cultural era would your spirituality best fit? • survival • medieval • modern • liminal			
Do you think secular fundamentalism exists?			
Do you seek a clear, easily understood, set of beliefs on which your spirituality is based?			
Is it important for you to feel the truthfulness of a person's belief?			
Could you summarize your spirituality in one word? In one sentence?			
Which of the following best describes your spirituality? • traditionalist • contemporalist • co-temporalist			

Questions	Reflections	Connections	Observations
• Does the Christian Bible contain all truth? • Is the Christian Bible inspired by God? • Is the Christian Bible without error? • Was Jesus born of a virgin? • Did Jesus perform miracles?			
Are the spiritual gifts central to your spirituality?			
Would you like to talk in tongues?			
Does your spirituality reflect any of the principles of the self-help movement?			
How important is the success and failure of your nation to your spirituality?			
What role do the sciences have in your spirituality—for example, cosmology, psychology, and sociology?			
Would you agree with, or modify, any of the principles advocated by the Unitarian Universalist Association as quoted in Chapter Four?			

Questions	Reflections	Connections	Observations
Do you believe that it is evident that religions change over time?			
Does anyone you know—friend or enemy—live a life reflecting traditionalist, contemporalist, or co-temporalist attitudes?			
Do you think traditioning is possible?			
Which of these themes are present in your spirituality? • consciousness, witness, verbalization • quick life change • Centrality of the individual person • distrust of institutions • conscious promotion of spiritual basics (survival spirituality) • new revelations • expert spiritual guides • shopping for a spirituality			

Questions	Reflections	Connections	Observations
Do you find any of the following paradigms as necessary for your spirituality? • nature • spirit • mind • totally different • action			

CHAPTER FIVE

CHOOSING AND EVALUATING YOUR SPIRITUALITY

It all comes down to motivation, doesn't it? It is hard work thinking and reflecting on your spirituality. It is not an easy task. Nor is it an easy task to change habits.

We've come to the end of your search. Now it is time to evaluate who you are and who you want to become, and to make choices to end your soul searching—for now.

First we will look at values in general and spiritual values in particular. Then we will talk about choosing and how to make your choices part of your life. Finally we will offer ways of evaluating your spirituality—past, present, and future.

Value

Value is a word we use to indicate that something is extremely important. It has many meanings in our society, but common to all of them is "importance." When we say these are our values, we are saying these are what are important to us. How do we know what is important to us? First let's look at what it's like when we do not have anything valuable in our lives.

Are Significant Values Present?

Ennui, boredom, alienation, and discomfort are all emotional indicators that your present values are absent or not functioning. From his experience in the Nazi concentration camps, Viktor Frankl argued that anyone who has a "why," a meaning in life, will find the "how" of living that life. Without a "why," we are bored. We have a sense that nothing is important. Nothing matters. Life is just one thing after another. To not be bored, Frankl argued, one must have values, for values pull us beyond ourselves. In going beyond ourselves, we grow, and in growing we deepen our identity and our joy of living.

Abraham Maslow suggested that a sense of ennui characterizes the person without values. This is someone who looks back at his or her life and can never point to a significant moment of wholeness. These significant moments of wholeness he calls a peak experience. Values encourage peak experiences. Without them we are just making it through life.

Extended use of the Purpose in Life Test, developed from the ideas of Frankl and Maslow, indicates that a failure to sustain a valuing life is associated with psychological alienation and discomfort. Certainly boredom, alienation, and discomfort will destroy any individual or group. How do we enliven ourselves and our communities? It is done by supporting the enhancement and development of the necessary spiritual values for wholistic living.

Are Our Values Imaginary or Real?

Many times when people talk about values, they talk about their hopes and their idealized principles of action. In stating their values, they realize that they seldom act on them. Such imaginary, or idealized, values may prompt us to act, but they are products of the mind. If we have many values and never act on them, or always falls short of our stated values, we must ask what we really consider important—what we really value. Our spiritual life is determined by our values. Values are the vector of what is important in our lives, what drives our lives forward, and what judges our everyday actions. Sometimes what we say are our values are actually our imaginary hopes.

How Do We Discern a Real Value?

Values are not "out there" waiting to be picked up like isolated pieces of gold or lovely flowers. Values are lived. We are valuing-people only if we associate with those who speak and act values. The sharing of values results in building good communities. Healthy communities share basic values and celebrate this sharing in symbolic acts, words, and deeds. We search for values individually and sometimes communally. We recognize our values by what we do. Values are ideals, words, and actions we choose, prize, and act on. We will look at these steps in more detail later in this chapter.

Our choosing may be in imitation of others in the socialization process. These kinds of values are part of us but usually we do not consciously choose them. Conscious choice is essential to valuing. For instance, many in our country have been brought up to treat others fairly. Fairness may even be seen as part of our American way of life. We may never have reflected on this value. Yet because of circumstances—we become a parent of five children, become a member of an affirmative action committee, or lose in an administrative competition to someone of a different race or gender—we have to reflect on what is fair. Actually, we define *fairness* in the way we respond to these situations, as we become conscious of the necessity for being fair and acting in fair ways. Conscious of fairness, we then decide whether it is for us or not. We choose to act fairly. We prize fairness when we publicly state its importance and act fairly. When we do this over and over, we can presume that it is a value. In acting fairly over a prolonged period, we establish the habit or virtue of fairness.

Does acting fair make us continually happy and result in enormous rewards? Of course not. But we're not bored! And, down deep, we have a sense of wholeness that sustains us in the midst of the controversies that surround our acting fair.

Real Values Are in a Set or Pattern

None of us has only one value. We have a set, or pattern, of values. This set of values is usually consistent from late teens until death. What varies is which value in the set provides primary direction to our complete set. The same can be said for a culture such as the United States. Thus, if Americans value private property, liberty, independence, usefulness, clear-cut moral imperatives, and choice as values in a value set, there may be times in which one of these rather than the other provides order to the set. Thus property may be more important than liberty; clarity of moral positions more important than choice.

A spiritual life is bound together by a set of values that we can see embodied in spiritual signposts as we go about our daily lives. In the spiritualities we have reviewed, we easily mistake the pivotal value of their set because our own pivotal value prevents us from seeing it. When our compass's north leads us one way, only discipline in the art of spiritual discernment allows us to see the alternative north(s) offered by these other spiritualities

Sets Operate According to Priorities That Vary According to Circumstances

Why does our priority of values shift? Because we are living creatures adapting to an ever-changing world in which we search for some still point to center our change. This adaptation, which is a response to the external changing environment, is also an adaptation to the internal necessities that govern the life cycle. We are constantly choosing, prizing, and acting. So a new choice of priorities results in a new direction of our spirituality. In other words, the set of values that has provided direction to our lives is still present, but now, because of external and/or internal circumstances, our lives take a new direction depending on our primary or pivotal value. Psychological maturity is the best determinant of what is leading our value choices. It is also one of the better determinants of what might be characterized as life-cycle spirituality.

Eric Erickson has provided us with an excellent way of describing a life-cycle spirituality. We begin life, Erikson suggests, with the tensions and challenges between trust and mistrust. If we experience consistent and continuous love in our early years, we probably become hopeful and mature. We also experience tensions and challenges between autonomy and doubt. If we have opportunities to try out new skills, we probably develop a mature will, because we will not be afraid of acting on our own. The ability to deal with these tensions and challenges at this stage of development enables us to enter into the next stage well prepared to meet its challenges. According to Erikson, this is the same with all subsequent stages.

Later in our childhood, tensions and challenges between initiative and guilt offer us an opportunity to accept life as purposeful. Solving the tensions and challenges between industry and inferiority during our school years allows us to have a sense of competence. If we have been praised for our appropriate actions, we will have this sense of accomplishment. The resolution of these tensions and challenges gives us a good start in facing the adolescent tensions and challenges between identity and role confusion. An ability to recognize continuity and sameness in our personalities in different situations and with different individuals enables us to know who we are without depending consistently on others for our identity and for approval of our actions. We can have a sense of fidelity to self and others as we have a sense of who we are.

Of course, knowing who we are isn't everything. How we interact with others is also a sign of maturity. A resolution of the tensions and challenges between intimacy and isolation in early adulthood leads to a mature ability to love. Gradually, we are able to fuse our identity with another in such a way that we are able to be intimate with other people.

Yet love is not everything. How do we compete with others? An overly competitive and combative relationship with others only leads to isolation. How do we face the tensions and challenges between becoming absorbed in ourselves and our own goals and being concerned with others? Solving these challenges results in either our being a caring person—one who can reach out and help others for their good and the good of the world—or being a narcissistic individual, only concerned with our own good.

Finally, all of us face the tensions and challenges of giving up hope in the face of suffering, injustice, and incomprehensible death. These tensions and challenges always surround us, but they begin to dominate much of our lives in the later years. To be able to face disintegration is to be wise. A mature older person is one who has the ability to look at her own disintegration of self and world and choose wholeness and life. This is wisdom.

This chart summarizes what we have seen so far.[24]

Pivotal Value (What's important)	Value Conflict	Vision of Self (How I feel)
Hope	trust vs. mistrust	Forming *There is more to life than I experience right now, and I can obtain it.*
Will	autonomy vs. reliance	Beginning recognition in things and others *I want to do it myself.*
Purpose	initiative vs. guilt	Inside/outside (fantasy) *I will do it myself.*
Competence	industry vs. inferiority	Action and friends *I can do it.*
Fidelity	identity vs. role confusion	Ideals *Doing it is part of who I am.*
Love	intimacy vs. isolation	Goals *Here I am. Treat me with care. We can and will do it.*
Care	generativity vs. self-absorption	Relationships *Look at what I/we did. Keep it going.*
Wisdom	integrity vs. despair	Memories *Everything is disintegrating. I'll keep it all together as long as I can.*

Maturity is never made in a moment nor celebrated by a birthday. Spiritual maturity, which has a value set composed of the values indicated by Erikson, is also not easily achieved. Maturity is a constant challenge of life: a challenge that never ends. We are always growing older. How we meet the above value conflicts determines our way of life. Each of us may be spiritually mature or immature depending on how we deal with these tensions and challenges.

If we begin life in a situation where we are not loved, where our pleas for warmth, for food, for cleanliness are not heard regularly, we will probably grow up not trusting our environment. The first stage of Erikson's theory suggests that if we do not experience trust in those first months of life, we will not be able to develop as a maturing person. From a Christian spiritual perspective, for example, we will have a difficult time accepting a trusting God or living a balanced spiritual life. If we never experience trust and love, we will never know the meaning of the symbols of love and trust. To describe a loving God, for example, is to describe a reality beyond our experience if we never knew human love. Our spiritual development is wholistic and thus always influenced by the way we are human.

However, developmental theory does suggest that we can "make up" or catch up on our development at a later stage. It is possible that during adolescence, for instance, we can struggle through trusting again. All the challenges of past stages of life can be relived and won at this stage of life.

The consequences of understanding developmental theory are many, but certainly one is an ability to understand the all-too-common experience of being bored with our everyday spiritual lives. Sometimes people find their church boring. – It is not responding to their concerns or even rejects what they hold dear. — It may be that in some of these situations our present developmental needs are in tension with those of the religious community into which we were socialized. A young family going to a church where everyone is over sixty cannot expect to share many of the same interests as their co-religionists. Many times our spiritual ennui is the result of those we associate with on a regular basis. If everyone in our niche has the same value set we do, but a different pivotal value, it can easily be that we have a sense of deep alienation without recognizing it. It is not us or the classical spiritual way of life that is causing the feeling, but instead the fact that there is no community support for where we are at in the spiritual life cycle. We must set about choosing either a more supportive community, new values for our set of values, or a pivotal value more in accord with our stage of life.

Choosing Our Values

When we congratulate individuals for a job well done or punish them for harming another, we do so because they own their action. They chose to act this way rather than that way, and as a consequence of that choice; they accept the responsibility of that action. It is their act; they own it. Our legal, ethical, and everyday culture is founded on the responsibilities that are consequent on the theory of free choice. At the same time, we are surrounded by those who wish to control our choices to achieve their ends. Contemporary free choice must always be considered within the context of personal responsibility and communal control.

When we concede the necessity and the possibility of free choice in contemporary society, we also concede the responsibility that accompanies it. A spiritual life does not consist of freedom alone or choice alone, but in free choices that result in our acceptance of the responsibility for our actions. A free choice may be bad as well as good. Both make us who we are and shape our spiritual lives.

Choosing the Necessary Values for a Spiritual Life

The values that must be present in a spiritual life are those that make up our spiritual signposts (belief, ritual, moral imperatives, community, and transcendent desire) and our spiritual compass (beauty, truth, self-discipline, order/harmony, loving, doing, and togetherness). In one way or another, they make up our set, or pattern, of values. Their presence in our set is the result of our socialization process or of our conscious choices throughout our life cycle. We are always responsible for those values we consciously choose and usually responsible for the others as they come to consciousness.

Socialization Process and Lazy Values

Nature or nurture? This question is always asked when talking about development. To choose one or the other is too modern, too reductionist, too secular fundamentalist. Nature, nurture, and free choice make us who we are.

Certainly both nature and nurture contribute to our final choices. We make our choices because of both our genetic makeup and the people who influence us throughout our lives. These value choices are embedded in thoughts, ideas, ideals, words, and actions. Socialization is how this society of people influences our thinking and acting. It embeds language distinctions, such as body, soul, spirit, and mind, as well as languages that make no distinctions; moral understandings, such as karma or divine judgment; life goals, such as the kingdom of God or nirvana; and even time sensitivity, such "as my life is going somewhere" or "my life is illusion and best let it happen, because I can't do anything about it." It also embeds our values and value patterns with little reflection as to the consequences of what have now become important to us. These socially embedded determinants of what we feel and think are important are our lazy values.

Awakening to New Ways of Life and Lazy Values

Usually the only time conscious choice comes to the fore is when the behavior, feelings, norms, or ideas resulting from the socialization process are clearly challenged. Before the challenge, these lazy values are the habits that constitute our identity. The challenges to individual values, or patterns of values, are most evident in crises and most profound in slow contextual

140

change where one does not remember how the set of lazy values of one time shifted to another set at another time. Both value changes may lead to either an entirely new set of values (a Christian becomes a Buddhist) or a shift of a pivotal value and its expression (a right-to-life Christian only concerned with abortion becomes someone who becomes concerned about everyone's right to life, not only the fetus'/baby's).

Some authors use the term *conversion* for a sudden awakening to the dysfunctionality of a former way of life and the necessary values of another way of life. Usually sudden conversions are accompanied by a long, detailed story or confession describing how that former way of life led them astray in terms of their present or future one. What is certainly evident in both the story and the conversion experience is that they are the result of a conscious choice of thought, word, or action that was not present before this awakening moment. Also present are sets of lazy values both rejected and accepted that we become aware of only with the passage of time after the initiatory experience.

It takes a while to know the newly accepted modes of behavior, feelings, norms, and ideas relative to the signposts of belief, ritual, moral imperatives, and community life. Sometimes this is done somewhat easily as we become aware of these new signposts; sometimes not. In either case, new habits must be learned to accompany this new spiritual life. This may easily include new dietary norms as we move from a meat-eating spirituality to one that distains eating meat. It may include new challenges to our sexual practices as we move from one set that easily accepts the use of contraceptive methods to another in which they are prohibited. It may include worship services held whenever we wish at a shrine rather than on one day a week with the same community. Changing habits is hard, especially as the months and years pass after the initiatory experience and subsequent choices. These changing habits bring to the fore not only the conscious choice of a way of life but also all the habits that are part of that new way and the values these habits demonstrate.

Changing Values and Hard Choices: Conversations with Your Self and Others

Habits express our values. The feelings we have associated with our habits help build and destroy both habits and values. As our surroundings change, so do our feelings, values, and habits. We must pay attention to all of these if we are to understand and change our spiritual values

Feelings that move us toward change are those associated with the root fears we described as part of the spirituality compass: boredom, grief, loneliness, chaos (confusion), pain (losing self-control), ignorance, and the unattractiveness of everything around us. As one or some of these feelings intensify, there is a perceived need to deal with them. In a pluralistic society, there are many offering ways to deal with this hurt that digs deep into our very existence and identity. Ideologies, drugs, alcohol, self-help programs, counselors, therapists, and volunteer opportunities are some of the avenues we may walk to care for our hurts.

Positive feelings also lead us to change our lives. An important idea, an opportunity to be part of a vital community, and a request to use our skills and knowledge to help those in need may lead us to change. The most recognized reason for change in spiritualities is marriage. These feelings and love of another human being lead us to individual patterns of change in our spiritual values.

External factors also come into play that urge us to change spiritualities. Sometimes this happens in ways we do not at first recognize, such as moving to a new part of the country or world where core values we took for granted at home no longer apply. New technologies, war, changing economic fortunes, environmental change, and shifting political majorities have significant influences on an individual's values and can cause shift in pivotal values. For example, one could not have as a pivotal Christian value the reading of the Bible until Bibles became available (printing) and people could read (education for all). The same question of value holds for people in oral cultures who have no written language. We cannot value what we do not have. We can hope, but values are what we actually hold as important: what we select, prize, and act on. Until the technology is developed, one may hope to read a Bible, but it is not actually a value. It is never a question of values or no values. It is always a question of which values one has within the dominant value pattern of society and one's unique spirituality.

Hard Choices: The Conditions

Several conditions have been found significant in helping people change and or deepen their spiritual life:

Motivation. The difficult question of "why" you want to do this must be answered. In answering it, you may discover other reasons, but you will also discover the core motivating factor for what you are doing. It may be as simple as "I love him" to a more complex "To better the lives of those in need" to "I want to discover my destiny."

- *Communal support.* Certainly isolated holy people walk the streets of our cities, whether in New York or New Delhi. But they are unique in living lives without the support of others. If you look more closely, even they depend on others for sustenance or recognition as being a holy person. "Self" and "others" are essential for living in general and spiritual living in particular.
- *Repetition.* Habits become habits by doing the behavior, feeling, thinking, and normative living over and over. With a set of habits, a spirituality develops.
- *Positive and negative reinforcement.* As you do the right thing over time, you should have a sense of purpose and a positive attitude about yourself. Instances of failing to behave think, and feel based on the new value(s) should result in negative feelings of guilt, uneasiness, and failure. These positive and negative repercussions to your newly chosen life and value set

are indicators of a developing spirituality. The goal is to build your life around these chosen values.

- *Distance from the previous environment* (physically, mentally, or socially) provides the space to be your new self. How to do it and the consequences of distancing yourself from previous habits usually includes distancing yourself from those who shared these habits with you. New values lead to developing a new self, and with the new self, new relationships. It is a challenge to keep both old and new together. But it can be done. In doing so, it may be your opportunity to love others as they are, while developing into someone different. In the beginning, when trying to develop a new set of values and spiritual life, it is best to put some distance between you and your former life.

- *Time.* Change takes time. Americans are always demanding instant solutions to organic problems. The only instant solution to something or someone that is growing is to kill it/him. Otherwise, it takes time to grow, to mature, and to interact with all the necessary realities that will make us who we are.

Hard Choices: The Process

If these are the conditions that enable you to implement the choices you make, the paradigm for making choices should be acknowledged. It is simply: select, prize, and act. In more detail, this paradigm may be described in the following steps. Remember that when we are talking about values here, we are not talking about abstractions but embodied values in thought, word, and deed. Here is the way this may look in daily life.

- *Dream, hope, imagine, experience, and remember.* From these you build a treasury of values from which you may choose at the opportune time.

- *Make a point of selecting values you both want to bring into your life and can reasonably expect to act on at this time.* If you are just beginning to change your spirituality, it is important to experience some initial success in making such a change. Such success is best had by making the easy changes first.
- *Think through the consequences of such choices.* This may be a practice in imagination, since much of what you expect may not happen, but it does dress the choice in an atmosphere of reality.
- *Take steps to change your life in clear accord with the newly adapted values.* Act on your values and begin the repetition necessary to move from the hope of making something or someone important to actually making it so.
- *Publically act and speak in accord with these values.*

The process of helping someone else make and sustain spiritual values is somewhat the same as when doing it yourself. Both processes follow the basic model of all value choice: select, prize, and act. If you are helping someone else, here is a brief recipe for doing so.

- Encourage the person to make choices and to make them freely.
- Help the person to discover and examine available alternatives when faced with choices.
- Help the person to weigh alternatives thoughtfully and to reflect on the consequences of each.
- Encourage the person to consider what he or she prizes and cherishes.
- Give the person opportunities to make public affirmations of the choices made.
- Encourage the person to act, behave, and live in accordance with the choices made.

- Help the person to examine repeated behaviors and life patterns (virtues) in relation to the choices he or she has made.
- Console in failure; encourage in success; remain a friend.

Hard Choices: The Substance

Judging between illusion and reality is difficult yet necessary. Snow White learned the hard way that because something looks like a red, nutritious, edible apple, does not mean it is edible. People who invested with Bernie Madoff learned that because their friends told them about a great investment and they trusted Mr. Madoff, it did not mean it was a good investment.

Actual, real change is many times in the eye of the beholder. Spiritual change is no different. Spiritual life is real life. Not opinionated life. Not irresponsible life. Not feelings alone. It is whole. It is real. When the values and the ideas, words, and actions that constitute one's spiritual life change, that change has real consequences on the individual and society.

When change is occurring in the signposts of your spiritual life, and you are not consciously aware of the change, you may be feeling bad and not know why. When that change is occurring among many people, an entire society may be doing and feeling certain ways and not know why. You may see examples of this change in many ways. For example, people can proclaim and deeply believe that they believe in God, the Father Almighty. The words may be the same; the feeling of belief may be the same. But is the substance of the belief and words the same as it was in 100 CE? In 100 CE, the science of the time said the total potentiality of the human was in the male sperm and the woman was passive; above the clouds was the perfect heavens; the power of the warrior's arm and sword was the best means to change history. In the twenty-first century, biological science provides evidence that both male and female are essential to the beginning of human development and that telescopes and travel to the moon have not found evidence of any physically divine-inhabited space. Today many people plead for change by peaceful means rather than coercive force. The same can be said of marriage in 100 CE, when it was often an exchange of property and talk of marriage rights and duties among diverse families. In 2012 CE marriage is primarily seen as two people deeply in love promising to continue that love forever in a tight bond of friendship, care, and concern. Some things may seem like they have not changed (the word *God,* and marital life) but substantively they have. They may look the same in both eras (the word *G-o-d,* two human beings) but they mean and function differently in the two.

People frequently experience the emotions associated with change, such as boredom, ignorance, and loneliness, without realizing that substantive change has occurred. They do not know why they feel the way they do. So, they deal with their feelings through substance abuse, mutual alienation, scapegoating, increased following of charismatic leaders, and/ or a shrinking vision of what is acceptable to self and society. Deep change has occurred, but because they see, hear, and act as they have in the past, they think nothing has happened. In fact it has.

Hard Choices: The More Things Change the More They Are the Same

We have described, reviewed, and analyzed many spiritualities with long histories. They exist today with claims of continuity and authenticity to things that were said and done thousands of years ago. Some adherents have reflected deeply on their present connection with their past origins and development; some have not. Those who have not are satisfied that they are an ancient spirituality, providing the promises and means of transcendence that have enlivened millions throughout time.

Millions today may have the feelings associated with value loss, but the leaders and thinkers in these classic traditions focus their attention on what is highlighted by the enthusiasms, both good and bad, that are stimulated by their present social, ideological, technological, and cultural environment. Scapegoating the present, they look to their sense of a common tradition to provide them with an identity and a promise of a better future devoid of the present environment. Other thinkers within these spiritualities go to great pains to demonstrate that their spirituality is doing now exactly what was done at its beginnings. Here are a few examples: Sacraments are signs instituted by Christ, so doing them, you do what Jesus did. Chants are found in the *Vedas*, so chanting them is doing what has been done by Hindus for millennia. Visiting the shrine at Ise has been done for millennia. So when I go there today, I am doing exactly what was done two thousand years ago. Literal imitation demonstrates that this is really so to these thinkers. Other thinkers carefully detail how things said and done at one time were "really" the same as we are doing today. So "God" was "always" understood as all-powerful, all-knowing, and just.

Essentially, there is no difference. The incidentals of cultural interpretations—of how a baby is made, that the universe is inhabited, or how people are influenced to do good—are incidental to the reality behind these descriptions. The reality is that God *is* who God *is*: the creator, the all-powerful and all-knowing director of history. These thinkers have provided a spirited defense that things are the same because the words and/or actions are the same, or that the essence of what is done, no matter what the change, is somehow the same, even though one is not doing exactly what was done before.

When making individual choices, these claims by religious experts sometimes are not enough. How do I know that this is the right one for me if I cannot rely on identity as a means of authenticity? How do I know whether I am being misguided by the loud shouts of approval and disapproval that mark thought and action in contemporary life? How do I know my present or hoped-for spirituality has substance—is true?

Your answers to these questions may follow the stages offered by Kohlberg: I feel this is the right thing to do or believe because such action and/or belief gives me pleasure; it is what all my friends do or believe, or everyone does or believes; it is authenticated as true by authorities independent of pleasure-pain or majority opinion. In the light of Kohlberg, we realize that the use of each one of these questions as the definitive norm coincides with one's maturation process. At the same time, they may also be seen as true when normed against the answers to the following questions.

- Is it reasonable? Does it fulfill the conditions of deductive and inductive reasoning?
- Does it agree with the tradition of your spiritual community?
- Is it supported by an authority in what you are deciding? (His or her learning and experience affirm your decision as the right one, or the expert is an authority because his or her religious role affirms this decision is correct.)
- Does it feel correct and safe? Is it pleasurable? Will I get hurt?

If you answered yes to three of these questions, you can be reasonably sure that your spirituality is developing in the proper direction.

Truth does not exist separate from those who speak it, hear it, and live it. Questions about living our spiritual truth must be asked. As with the questions above, the answer "yes" or an affirmative response to a choice indicates that you are on the road to deepening your spiritual life. A "no," or negative response to a choice, should make you stop and reevaluate what exactly causes such a response. Talking to someone knowledgeable about the spiritual life should help you see the choices you must make to continue your spiritual development.

- Does it destroy or deepen your relationship with others?
- Does it form or deform the life you live with others?
- Does it contribute to your personality development?
- Does it improve your ability to live creatively with ambiguity, uncertainty, and chaos?
- Does it lead you to engage with some of the foundational questions of life—questions of justice, of peace, of health, of responsibility, of belonging, of meaning?
- Does it help you love and live better?

- Does it intensify those values that are appropriate to where you are in your life cycle?

Summary

Your values—what are important to you—tell you who you really are. What your spirituality envisions as your road to transcendence tells you who you wish to become. The importance of "now" is challenged by the importance of the envisioned "not yet." Choosing carefully; building habits securely ensures your arrival at what you wish to become.

Simple questions and simple answers do not complete the embracing wholeness of a spiritual life. Transcending life's boundaries always leaves behind the memory of the transcending experience and the inherent boundaries of life's deep mystery. The sharp distinctions inherent in well-reasoned analysis always leave behind what reason cannot embrace. The exhilarating emotions touching the edges of each sense stop, because they cannot touch, smell, hear, taste, and see beyond the material world they enliven.

A spirituality seeks satiation to transcendent desire—final answers to abiding questions. We dive deep into mystery for satisfaction and answers. Well-worn signposts offer a path. Within us a yearning for truth, justice, beauty, togetherness, health, meaningful activity, and direction provide the breath of life in mystery's depths as we seek a true path to discover completeness.

Completeness "now" is still "not yet." "Now" is the promise embedded in the thought, the ritual, the authentic and just action, the bond with another, the experience that touches us and pulls us forward. "Not yet" is the promise's fulfillment. We live in now-not-yet. Our developing spirituality is at one time like a strong, rushing river that embraces all in its path; at another, it is a calm pond reserved for just us to slowly, very slowly, enter until encompassed by its warm wetness. But it is ours. It is yours. Live it. Never abandon its promise, for it will be fulfilled. You will find your soul.

DEAR DIARY V

WHAT'S BEST FOR ME?

Lawrence Kohlberg, following Jean Piaget, says that we answer the question "What's best for me?" differently throughout out life: What gives me pleasure. What my friends say is best. What logically fulfills my needs. Diverse businesses daily tell us what is best for us through advertising. Usually they appeal to our pleasurable wants and desires for power, food, sex, and comfort. Judaism, Christianity, and Islam teach that God knows what is best, since we are creatures. Follow God's revelation as offered by God's people, and the kingdom will come, heaven will be realized. Taoism and Confucianism teach that whatever brings harmony among us is what is best. Using correct manners and thoughts will bring humanity peaceful existence. Hinduism and Buddhism show that what is best is beyond imagination, illusion, desire, and suffering. Practice the proper yoga, and nirvana will result.

You have finished your review of your past. Now is the time to choose—to do what is best for the soul that you are. You will be aided in making your choices by first reviewing your values with an emphasis on your moral signpost; then going back over your "Dear Diary" writing to make selections for the future; and finally sketching your spiritual choices for the future.

What Is Important To Do? What Is Important To Avoid?

Questions	Observations	Connections	Reflections
Should what you eat or not eat reflect your spiritual principles?			
Do you avoid certain food and drink?			
Do you fast on certain days?			
Should your sexual relations be guided by your spiritual principles?			
What role does gender play in your sexual relations?			
Do you believe that regulation of birth is necessary in this world?			

Questions	Observations	Connections	Reflections
Do you believe that it is necessary to give pleasure to your partner both in sexual intercourse and throughout the day?			
Is it important to who you are to be concerned about those in need?			
Is it necessary to care for the natural environment?			
Is it necessary that our economy grow?			
Is interest on loans a spiritual issue?			
Is it necessary to avoid war? What is your role in advocating for or against war?			

Questions	Observations	Connections	Reflections
Do you consider the following to be dysfunctional to your spiritual life? • lust • pride • gluttony • sloth • envy • anger • avarice			
• Do you worship God? • Do you avoid idols of all sorts? (Idols = giving ultimate importance to beliefs, rituals, morals, and communities not a part of your spirituality) • Do you insult God and God's creation?			

Questions	Observations	Connections	Reflections
• Do you regularly gather with those who follow your spirituality? • How do you treat your parents? • Do you believe you shouldn't kill any human person? Any animal? Any organism? • Do you steal? • Do you lie? • Are you envious of the people you work with or live near?			
Should you do everything possible to live? This includes operations, medicine, and spending of money as well as taking pain relief?			

Questions	Observations	Connections	Reflections
Answer the following true or false: • Nature is not real; it is an illusion caused by our own ignorance and/or desires. • Nature is a means of bringing compassion to all living beings. • Nature is essential to life, for it is part of the ever-changing process in which the harmony and unity of life's mystery is present. • Nature is the means through which the power of invisible forces comes into our lives. • Nature is real and necessary for us to bring all animate and inanimate things into harmony with each other.			

Questions	Observations	Connections	Reflections
Who do you value?			
Look back at Erickson's chart in Chapter Five. Using the numbers 1-7, with one being the most important, prioritize this list of values.			
Name five people, things, animals, or institutions you are responsible for?			
Can you name three things that were valued by • your parents? • your two best friends? • your two worst enemies?			
How do your values clarify your desire for transcendence? How do your values help satiate your desire for transcendence?			

Going Back to Go Forward

I have said that a spiritual life promises and promotes the vision and means to change the present into another, better world in the near or distant future, and that a spirituality is a way of life that seeks a beneficial transformation and transcendence of self and community. From what you have said in your previous "Dear Diary" sections, respond to the following questions using the coding system below.

Mark a **B** next to anything that reflects your current beliefs.

- Mark a **R** next to anything that reflects your current ritual expressions.
- Mark a **M** next to your current moral imperatives (what to do/avoid) in bringing about transcendence for yourself and all humanity.
- Mark a **C** next to those you claim as your spiritual comrades.
- Mark a **Cu** next to the culture in which your current spirituality would best be lived.
- Mark a **T** next to anything and anyone you are thankful for.

Answer the following questions.

- Do you have a mechanistic or organic view of yourself and your spirituality (Chapter Four)?
- Are any themes and paradigms (Chapter Four) present in your spirituality?
- What does your spirituality promise to achieve?
- What beliefs, ritual, moral imperatives, and community does it provide to support that promise?
- Does it accept the paradoxes of Chapter Two?

- What is one thing that has to change to improve your spiritual life?
  - o How does it relate to your spiritual compass?
  - o How does it relate to your spiritual signposts, especially your close relationships?
  - o How does it promise and promote transcendence in your spiritual life?

Describe how you expect your spiritual life to be once you have adapted the above change by making it a habit.

Will this envisioned spiritual life:

- Destroy or deepen your relationship with others?
- Form or deform the life you live with others?
- Contribute to your personality development?
- Improve your ability to live creatively with ambiguity, uncertainty, and chaos?
- Lead you to engage with some of the foundational questions of life—questions of justice, of peace, of health, of responsibility, of belonging, of meaning?
- Help you love and live better?
- Intensify those values that are appropriate to where you are in your life cycle?

MAY YOUR FUTURE BE BETTER THAN YOUR PRESENT AND MAY YOUR SOUL BE EVER ALIVE AMID THE MYSTERY AND PARADOXES OF LIFE.

APPENDIX A:

THREE FOUNDATIONAL CULTURES

	Medieval	Modern	Liminal
Norm	That which we have done before that resulted in survival	That which is logical, scientifically proven, rational and results in economic security	That which provides an experience capable of being repeated and results in well-being.
Dominant mode of elites' reasoning.	Deductive & a priori	Inductive and a posteriori with an emphasis upon the method to be used for both modes of reasoning.	Dialectical & wholistic
Work	Farmer (Hunter, gatherer)	Industry	Technological, Information
Organization	Inherited or "ordained" status	Rational bureaucratic authority	Teams and transitional gatherings of professionals for immediate goals and objectives

	Medieval	Modern	Liminal
Government	Feudal	Strong central bureaucracy	Democratic/ populist, declining emphasis upon authority, (church /state) for policy making but continually responsive to power groups capable of providing celebrity and populist experiences
Distrust	The new, the outsider, unbridled reason and analysis	The old, supernatural norms and experience	The boring and abstract, unbridled science; normative (religion) producing uniformity
Dominant Status	"Religious" - like God-speaker/ actor, E.g. pope, king.	Scientist (e.g. doctor) as objective discoverer of truth.	Celebrity - providers of well-being

	Medieval	Modern	Liminal
Core values	Sharing, work, loyalty	Individual accumulation, hard work differentiation, choice, pluralism, relativity, reductionism, empirical (rational), this worldly. It is dominated by instrumental and pragmatic reasoning and usually demeans tradition.	Leisure, individual self-expression, quality of life concerns
God	As king	As machine	As love
Threat to status quo	Occult: dark and hidden works of the devil	Parapsychology	Absolutes, norms and acknowledged limits

	Medieval	Modern	Liminal
Vision of Universe	The earth in the center surrounded by spheres of perfect circles which are the stepping stones to heaven, the farthermost sphere. Some retained a biblical view of the universe with the earth as the center and God in the clouds above earth.	The sun is the center of the solar system. Established upon the laws discovered by Kepler and Newton, seen by people like Galileo, the Copernican revolution changed how humans understood themselves in the universe.	No center as demonstrated by the relativity of Einstein, the observations of Shapely, the Doppler Effect and the Big Bang theory.
Power	Coercive as local or transcendent. The transcendent is available to all but many times controlled by clergy.	Coercive, usually associated with mechanical; elicitive associated with professional knowledge; leaders.	Although the total destruction of the human universe is possible through human weapons the day to day life of the liminal universe favors the elicitive power of choice over coercive power.

Appendix B

Key Facts for Classical Spiritualities

Schema for understanding a Spirituality

SPIRITUALITY and RELIGION	PLACE OF ORIGIN	MEMBERSHIP	KEY DATES	CENTRAL PERSON	BOOKS
CORE ISSUE Foundational Evil that prevents the fulfillment of the promise.	BELIEFS Descriptive stories, beliefs, songs, and words that are normative for describing and bringing about the promise.	RITUALS Repeated words and actions that help fulfill the promise	MORALS What is considered right or wrong; what helps fulfill the promise.	ORGANIZATION. Polity, how the spiritual community comes together or is divided. Those who help one fulfill the promise.	PROMISE Complete transcendence for the individual.

SPIRITUALITY and RELIGION	PLACE OF ORIGIN	MEMBERSHIP	KEY DATES	CENTRAL PERSON	BOOKS
JUDAISM	MESOPOTAMIA/ PALESTINE	World membership is one of the smallest; North America, second largest.	+/- 1700 Origins 1200 Exodus 597-538 Exile 70 CE Jerusalem destroyed. 1948 State begins	Abraham 18th Moses 12 th David 10th century BCE.	The Tanakh: Compilation begins in 12th century BCE; finalized 1st century CE

CORE ISSUE	BELIEFS	RITUALS	MORALS.	ORGANIZATION.	PROMISE
How can we live a good life? Acts contrary to the covenant	Torah. YAHWEH (YHWH). People of God. Kingdom of God.	Seasonal and life cycle rites. Sabbath. Circumcision.	Mitzvah (613 for men). Torah. 10 Commandments.	Synagogue. Orthodox. Conservative. Reformed.	Kingdom of God.

SPIRITUALITY and RELIGION	PLACE OF ORIGIN	MEMBERSHIP	KEY DATES	CENTRAL PERSON	BOOKS
CHRISTIANITY	PALESTINE (Jerusalem, Nazareth)	Largest in the world and in the United States.	25 Origins 1054, Division of Catholics and Orthodox 1517: Division Catholics and Protestants 19 th century Evangelical movement 20th century Pentecostal movement	JESUS 4 BCE-30 CE)	The Bible: Old Testament Tanakh); New Testament; Apocrypha. N.T. begins compilation 50 and list complete by 4th century

CORE ISSUE	BELIEFS	RITUALS	MORALS	ORGANIZATION.	PROMISE
Following Jesus' way of life. Sin and free will.	God: Creator, Redeemer, and Sanctifier. Jesus. Grace. People of God.	Lifecycle and seasonal rites. Sacraments or Ordinances. Saints. Sunday.	Sermon on the Mount; 10 commandments. Prayer, fasting, almsgiving.	Eastern Orthodox. Roman Catholic. Protestant Church. Monasteries	Kingdom of God. Heaven

SPIRITUALITY and RELIGION	PLACE OF ORIGIN	MEMBERSHIP	KEY DATES	CENTRAL PERSON	BOOKS
ISLAM	ARABIAN PENINSULA	Second largest in the world and third largest in North America.	570-632, Origins 630-1492, Growth 18th century: beginning of colonization	MUHAMMAD 570-632 CE	The Qur'an begun 610 CE; finalized 632 CE.
CORE ISSUE	BELIEFS	RITUALS	MORALS	ORGANIZATION.	PROMISE
Primacy of God and obeying God's will as in the Quran.	Allah. Qur'an. Universal Brotherhood	Friday. Lifecycle and season rituals. Ramadan.	Five Pillars. Hajj.	Mosque Shiite Sunni Sufis	Heaven.

SPIRITUALITY and RELIGION	PLACE OF ORIGIN	MEMBERSHIP	KEY DATES	CENTRAL PERSON	BOOKS
HINDUISM	INDIA	Fourth in the world. Among the smallest in North America	2750 BCE, 1175, 1690, 1947 CE		Rig Veda (Vedas) 1500; Upanishads 800-400 BCE; The Bhagavad-Gita 500-200 CE.
CORE ISSUE	BELIEFS	RITUALS	MORALS	ORGANIZATION.	PROMISE
Desire as formative of the conscious self. (Ignorance & Illusion).	Karma, Rebirth, Liberation/escape. (Moksha). One eternal self who we are. Atman is Brahman.	Home altar & Punja. Devotion to gods & goddesses. Life cycle. Meditation. Chants. Mantra.	Kama (pleasure), Artha (wealth) Duty (Dharma) to the proper order of things. Mosha (liberation) Caste. No: meat, fish, eggs, alcohol, gambling, illicit sex…	Caste (Jati) Temples	Liberation, escape from this Illusionary life.

SPIRITUALITY and RELIGION	PLACE OF ORIGIN	MEMBERSHIP	KEY DATES	CENTRAL PERSON	BOOKS
BUDDHISM	INDIA	Fifth largest in the world. Among the smaller groups in North America	563-483, 220-552 BCE: 749, 1175 CE.	SIDDARTHA GAUTAMA 563 (BCE) (BUDDAHA)	The Dhammapada

CORE ISSUE	BELIEFS	RITUALS	MORALS	ORGANIZATION.	PROMISE
Suffering. Because our conscious self is the result of craving and delusion.	Anatman: no eternal self, all is change. Rebirth. Nirvana.	Yogas......	Five precepts Eightfold path.	Theravada Mahayana Vajrayana	Nirvana.

SPIRITUALITY & RELIGION	PLACE OF ORIGIN	MEMBERSHIP	KEY DATES	CENTRAL PERSON	BOOKS
CONFUCIANISM	East Asia (China)	Sixth largest in the world. One of the least represented in North America.	551–479 BCE,	MASTER KUNG (CONFUCIUS)	The Analects of Confucius
CORE ISSUE	BELIEFS	RITUALS	MORALS	ORGANIZATION.	PROMISE
Disharmony – especially among classes of people.	Each works for the whole. Ideal person.	Li (Good form, courtesy)) all the correct rites and rituals proper to your role in society. Ancestor worship, spirit worship.	Inner & outer virtues. Jen (humaneness). Shu (reciprocity). Hsueh (self-correcting wisdom).	Shrines	Harmonious Society.

171

SPIRITUALITY & RELIGION	PLACE OF ORIGIN	MEMBERSHIP	KEY DATES	CENTRAL PERSON	BOOKS
TAOISM	East Asia (China)	Same as Confucianism.	604 BCE	LAO TZU (604 BCE)	Tao Te Ching
CORE ISSUE	BELIEFS	RITUALS	MORALS	ORGANIZATION.	PROMISE
Disharmony in self, nature, and among people.	Yin (dark) and Yang (bright) forces or energies. Tao. Resist permanence.		Te (virtuous life). Wu wei (non-purposiveness). "..in letting go all gets done." Be rooted in the Tao.	Shrines	Harmony with Tao.

Comparing Buddhist Spiritualities

	Theravada	Mahayana	Vajrayana
Origins	483 C.E.	500 CE	700 CE
Also known as	School of the Elders	The Great Vehicle Chan, Tendai, Pure Land, Zen, Nichiren	Tibetan, Tantric, Diamond Vehicle, Tantrayana, Mantrayana, Shinogon
Inherent to (Minor influence in India after 250 BCE	India, Siri Lanka, South East Asia	India, East Asia,	India, Tibet, East Asia
Buddha is	Siddhartha Gautama, the enlightened one	Cosmic Siddhartha Gautama	One of many male and female cosmic Buddhas.

	Theravada	Mahayana	Vajrayana
Texts	Pali Canon	Lotus Sutra, Diamond Sutra, are two of many	Most are transmitted orally. *Bardo Thodol* (The Tibetan Book of the Dead)
Pivotal Concern	Enlightenment	Compassion	The power of enlightenment. (Vajrayana: The Diamond or Thunderbolt Vehicle)
Present model of human perfection.	Arhat: One who has followed the Buddha in the Middle way of dedication to the dharma.	Bodhisattva: the sharing in the compassionate empowering of self end others in their Buddha nature.,	Lamas: one who possesses special magical powers revealing them as Buddha and bodhisattva.

Appendix C

Dos and Don'ts of Spiritual Listening

Dos

- Prepare by learning about spirituality, particularly the signposts and how they affect a person's spiritual perspective.
- Learn to recognize religious emotions such as the sacred, the supernatural, the mystical, loyalty, devotion, obedience, and justice.
- Protect the environment of the encounter with the other.
- Listen and be sensitive first to the emotions, then the words, and finally the meaning of what is said.
- Nurture the moment within a memory of the past and a hope for the future.
- Listen to what is valuable to, of, and for the other.
- Establish an atmosphere of mutual concern.
- Stick to the basics.
- Keep in mind that while concentrating on listening to one person, someone else is not being attended to.
- Life is more important than listening; remove yourself from dangerous situations.
- Reflect on the event as soon as possible afterwards and record your reactions to what you have heard and what you have not heard.
- Change takes time.
- Act on what you hear.

Don'ts
Interrupt, give advice, jump to conclusions, or argue.
- Demean or turn away from the other mentally or physically.

- Embody negative attitudes toward the other.
- Be too active (instead, just be present; don't spoil the atmosphere; let it become).
- Be troubled by silence.
- Be upset by embarrassment.
- Be frightened by overwrought religious emotions.
- Be afraid of the unknown.
- React quickly unless in danger.
- Expect too much.

GLOSSARY

Agnosticism: a belief that you cannot prove that God exists

Ahimsa: a Sanskrit-derived word meaning to avoid all harm. Usually translated "to do no harm" to any living thing (do not kill). This is part of the belief system of Hindus, Buddhists, and Jainists.

Ali: the husband of Fatima, Mohammad's daughter, was fourth Caliph. His death is seen as the beginning of Shite Islam since he was seen as the true successor to Mohammad.

Allah: the Arabic word for God

Amaterasu: Shinto goddess of the sun worshiped at the Ise shrine since the seventh century. The Japanese emperor is believed to be a direct descendent of Amaterasu.

Amitabha: the celestial Buddha of Mahayana Buddhism

Analects, the (ca. 475- 221 BCE): a collection of Confucius' sayings by his close disciples

Anatman (no atman): the Buddhist belief that no permanent, substantial, self exists

Anicca: the Buddhist belief that everything is always changing

Animism: the belief that everything is a living, willful, intelligent entity

Apocalypse: a description of total destruction, usually of the earth. In the Roman Catholic Bible, it is another word for the Book of Revelation or a type of storytelling within the Bible.

Arhant (Arhat): a Buddhist title for one who has attained Nirvana

Asceticism: a principled way of life designed to control one's mental and bodily desires

Ashkenazim: Jews who lived or came from Europe and Russia

Atheism: a belief that God does not exist

Atman: the Hindu word for the breath, soul, spirit, and the true self that you are

Auditing: the process in scientology of asking a series of questions put to the ones being audited in order to clear them of all barriers so that they may realize their true identity

Avalokitesvara: the one who embodies the compassion of Buddha

Avatar: In Hindism, this refers to the incarnation of one of the deities, usually Vishnu, Shiva, or Ganesha.

Avidya: In Hindu belief, this is the means by which a human being naturally mistakes that which is unified as being diversified.

Bar Mitzvah: the coming of age ceremony of a young Jewish male

Bat Mitzvah: the coming of age ceremony of a young Jewish female (not held in the Orthodox community)

Bhagavad Gita (Gita): The "song of god" is a Sanskrit text providing the revelations of the god Krishnathat he exists within each of us, and the means to realize this presence in its entirety.

Bhakti yoga: a way of devotion for gaining freedom from samsara

BibleBelieving Christians: those Christians who accept the literal reading of the Christian Bible as the sole norm of faith, science, and daily living. The current reading of the Bible and the preaching of charismatic individuals provide the normative expression of Jesus's way of life.

Bodhisattva : the process and/or consequence of enlightenment in Mahayana Buddhism; someone who has attained Buddhahood

Brahma: the Hindu god of creation

Brahman (Brahmin): ultimate reality; the mystery of life

Buddha (the enlightened one): anyone who has attained perfect enlightenment; usually in reference to Siddhartha Gautama, the supreme Buddha

Bushido: the title given to the way of life of the Japanese samurai

Cabala (Kabbalah): a marginal perspective on the relationship between humans and the universe. Originating and still in existence within Judaism, the written materials foundational to cabalistic teaching have been used by many marginal spiritualities as instruments of instruction and ritual within their own unique spirituality. These interpretations are significantly different from those within the Jewish tradition.

Caliph: the leader of the Muslim Ummah (community) and successor to Mohammed

Canon: the normative writings of a religion and/or spirituality

Caste (Varnas): the four ancient divisions of Hindu society that determine one's dharma. These were the teacher and priest caste (*Brahmana),* the warrior caste (*Kshatriya*), the farmer and trader caste (*Vasya*), and the caste of manual laborers (*Sudra*).

Catholic: usually refers to Roman Catholics, those Christians who accept the pope as their final authority in all matters and the successor of Peter the apostle. Some Christian churches also call themselves Catholic based on the original meaning of the term "universal."

Ch'an Buddhism (China): a variety of Mahayana Buddhism

Charism: Within Christianity, this term refers to a gift of God. One list is found in 1 Corinthians 12:8-8: wisdom, knowledge, faith, healing, miracles, prophecy, discerning spirits, tongues, and the interpretation of tongues.

Charismatic: As a general term, it refers to a person's ability to inspire others to thought and/or action. Within Christianity, it refers to one who has a charism (see above).

Christian Fundamentalism: In imitation of secular fundamentalism and founded upon the perspective of the Traditionalists, this way of life seeks the uniformity of literally derived beliefs, laws, and rituals from the Bible to build a society prepared for the Second Coming of Jesus Christ.

Christians: followers of Jesus, the Christ. Usually divided into Roman Catholic, Pentecostal, Protestant, Lutheran, Anglican, Presbyterian, Methodist, Evangelical, and Greek Orthodox. There are thousands of titles for communities who follow Jesus.

Chuang Tzu (Fourth Century BCE): a Chinese intellectual and thinker responsible for a foundational book of Chinese culture of the same name, Chuang Tzu

Classic Spiritualities: See *Glossary of terms for discussing spiritualities.*

Clear: a term in Scientology referring to the attainment of a state of mind devoid of emotions and thoughts that prevent one from making decisions helpful to her or his true Thetan nature.

Cleric: a member of the clergy

Confucius (551-479 BCE)/Great Master Kung/K'ung fu-tzu: a teacher and author who had a profound impact on Chinese culture. He detailed methods (virtues) for building a harmonious society.

Conservative Judaism: Jews who reject both Orthodox and Reform Judaism; Thus they observe some of the laws and have both English and Hebrew in their religious ceremonies.

Contemporalists: those who seek to harmonize the selected core values of the past with the central values of the modern and its technologies in order to change the present into a better future.

Conversion: moving from one spirituality to another with the understanding that the new spirituality provides you with the promise of final transcendence and the signposts to achieve it.

Co-temporalists: those who look to a literal imitation of the modern, manifested in the diverse sciences, as a way to transform the present world into a better one.

Coven: a community of witches

Covenant: the mutually binding promises made between God and the Jews in which God promises to watch over them forever and they promise to worship only God and follow his laws.

Cult: a marginal religious or spiritual group. Sometimes this is also used to refer to a mode of worship.

Dali Lama: the leader of the lamas in Yellow Hat Tibetan Buddhism. Tibetan Buddhists see him as the incarnation of compassion.

Demons: evil spirits who fight against the good spirits, especially God

Dharma (dhamma): first used in Hinduism to describe the proper order of both universe and society. Sometimes seen as the laws one must follow to obtain enlightenment.

Diaspora: the dispersal of people from their homeland. Many times this is used, in the West, in reference to the manner of Jewish migration from Israel, especially after 70 CE.

Doctrine: the teaching of a spirituality that is accepted as absolute truth

Dogma: a set of normative beliefs. In Roman Catholicism, dogma is the highest in a hierarchy of official beliefs.

Dualism: a vision of the world as radically divided in two, such as creator and created; good and evil.

Ecumenism: the movement within Christianity for greater unity in doctrine, ritual, moral norms, and polity; not to be confused with "interfaith," which refers to interchanges among diverse religions

Eightfold Path of Buddhism: This is a method of stopping desire through having the right views, right intention, right speech, right action, right livelihood, right effort, right mindfulness, and right concentration.

Enlightenment: an eighteenth century European movement emphasizing reason and the scientific method as the means for discovering truth

Enlightenment: the process and achievement of total transcendence within Buddhism usually resulting in Nirvana

Eschatology: the study of events surrounding the end of the world and the entire universe

Ethics: the study of what is right and wrong; good and bad; systems of morality

Evangelical: a protestant movement emphasizing personal salvation by Jesus, the centrality of the Bible, and the necessity of telling everyone about the good news that is Jesus.

Exodus: a central story in Jewish spirituality. It is the story of their leaving a life of slavery in Egypt to a life of freedom in the Promised Land.

Fakir: a Sufi Muslim beggar and mystic; also, a mendicant wonder worker in Hinduism

Feng-shui: Chinese practice of orienting buildings and plantings according to the energy lines present in the Tao.

Five Pillars of Islam: the foundational acts required to follow Allah's will—to believe that there is one Allah and Mohammad is God's prophet; daily prayers, almsgiving, fasting during Ramadan, and a pilgrimage to Mecca

Foundational Attitudes: meaning, belonging, purpose, and well-being. These are present in every form of spirituality.

Four Noble Truths of Buddhism: All life is suffering; the cause of suffering is desire (attachment); stopping desire will stop suffering; you stop desire by following the eightfold path.

Fundamentalism: See the definitions elsewhere in this list for secular fundamentalism and/or Christian or Muslim fundamentalism.

Gemara: rabbinic commentary on the Mishnah which, when combined with the Mishnah, are the Talmud.

Gita (Bhagavad Gita): The "song of god" is a Sanskrit text providing the revelations of the god Krishna, that he exists within each of us, and the means to realize this presence in its entirety.

Gnostics: In general, Gnostics claim a secret knowledge founded upon the experience of otherness of their body from their conscious spirit. The spirit is a remnant of the divine, now living in materiality. Gnosticism provides the methods for this divine spirit to return to its original spirit world.

Gospels (Good News): Accounts of Jesus's preaching, miracles, and life, usually in reference to the four gospels in the Christian New Testament: Matthew, Mark, Luke, and John.

Grace (gift): In Christianity, this designates God's gift of God's presence, mercy, and love to humankind. Christians have developed an intricate system of commentary around these gifts.

Guru (master, director): This term is typically used in reference to one who directs one's spiritual life in Hinduism.

Hadith: Mohammad's word and actions used to provide an understanding of God's revelation in the Quran.

Haggadah: the detailed description of the Jewish Passover ritual. Some Jews use this term for the actual Passover ritual.

Haij: the sacred and mandatory Muslim pilgrimage to Mecca in Saudi Arabia

Halakah: all Jewish law

Hassidic Judaism: a Jewish eighteenth century ultra-orthodox movement begun in Eastern Europe. It is characterized by ecstatic prayer and consciousness of God's continual presence. Their way of dressing, which reflects the style of dress worn at the time of their origin, makes them easily recognizable.

Hejira (hejira): the first year of the Muslim calendar, which began when Mohammed left Mecca for Medina in 622 CE

Horned god: one of the important gods in Wicca and other neo-pagan spiritualities; usually associated with sexuality and animality

I Ching (The Book of Changes): an ancient foundational text of Chinese spirituality that contains ways of understanding self and the future

Iblis: the devil in Islam

Idolatry: giving illicit primacy to things, people, and ideas; the worship of anything but God

Imam: an Islamic scholar of the Sharia; many times in the United States he is seen as the leader of a mosque

Immortality: living forever; usually before and after human bodily existence

Incarnation: in Christianity, the belief that Jesus is both God and human

Indigenous Spirituality: See "Key Terms for Discussing Spiritualities"

Instrumental values: those people and/or things that are a means to an end

Ise: the major shrine of Shinto spirituality

Jainism: followers of Nataputta Vardhamana (579-527 BCE) who advocate total non-violence

Jen: the virtue of "concern for others" in the spiritualities based on Confucius

Jihad (struggle): the command that a Muslim must do everything possible to live out his/her spirituality. Sometimes Jihad is understood as doing everything possible to defend the Muslim community from evil.

Jina (conqueror): the Jain description of enlightenment

Jinn: the Muslim designation of both good and evil spirits

Jiva: the self; in Jainism, the jiva is one's eternal soul; in Hinduism, one's temporal self.

Jnana yoga: the way of knowledge for gaining freedom from samsara

Kaaba (cube): The most sacred shrine of Muslims located in Mecca, which is composed of a large black rock cube and other items.

Kabbala: Originally an ancient Jewish method for understanding the Tanakh, it has become a method used by many marginal spiritualities to help understand the individual's relationship to the universe.

Kali : the "dark mother;" the goddess of death, destruction and renewal

Kami: the diverse beings and forces that inhabit Shinto spirituality

Karaism: a Jewish movement that rejects all subsequent legal authorities after the Tanakh

Karma yoga: the way of action for gaining freedom from samsara

Karma: the effect of our past actions upon our present role in the cycle of life and death (samsara)

Khalsa (pure): members of the Sikh military fraternity who wear the five Ks: *kesh*, uncut hair; *kangha*, comb; *kachh*, short pants; *kara*, steel bracelet; and *kirpan*, sword.

Kosher: Jewish dietary laws

Krishna: a Hindu god, considered by many to be an avatar of the god Vishnu, who plays a central role in the Bhagavad-Gita

Kuan-yin: a bodhisattva to East Asian Buddhists and an immortal to Taoists. To Buddhists, she is the goddess of mercy.

Lao Tzu (Old Master): the founder of Taoism and author of *Tao-te-ching*

Lent: a Christian time of fasting, prayer, and almsgiving lasting forty days—from Ash Wednesday to Easter Sunday

Li: The central virtue in Confucius's system because it is the sum of all virtues and thus demonstrates how one is to act in achieving a harmonious life. It is made up of all routine human interactions, from getting up in the morning to going to sleep at night; from eating breakfast to talking to one's parents.

Life's Mystery: the recognition that we are limited in every way yet yearn to go beyond those limits. It is the desire for more than the here-and-now and the conviction that there is a there-and-then.

Liminality: existing in between two modes of existence or, in this book, cultures. *Individual* liminality is living in between different identities and senses of self; communal or *cultural* liminality is existing in a time of uncertainty and distrust of politics, economics, language, and spiritualities. See *liminal spirituality* in *Glossary of Key Terms for Discussing Spiritualities*.

Lotus Sutra: Many times translated into English as the "Sūtra on the White Lotus of the Sublime Dharma," this ancient text is one of the most important for Mahāyāna Buddhism and several schools derivative from it.

Magic: may be understood in both a this-worldly and otherworldly sense. In essence, however, it consists of a ritual of words and actions to bring about a desired end. The conviction of the magician will interpret the nature and working of the ritual.

Mahayana Buddhism: most Buddhists adhere to this way of spirituality. It is called the "greater vehicle" because it is open to everyone, not just monks. Through the proper practice of compassion, anyone can become a Buddha.

Mantra: a word or group of words in Hinduism considered having power to shape one's spirituality

Marginal Spirituality: See the *Glossary of Key Terms for Discussing Spiritualities*.

Mecca: the holiest Muslim city and part of the obligatory pilgrimage, the *hajj*. It is the original home of Mohammed as well as where the Quran was written. It is in Saudi Arabia.

Medina: the place to which Mohammed fled and established the first Muslim community in 622 CE

Meditation: a term with unique meanings in diverse spiritualities. Common to all is the necessity for deliberate and concentrated focus upon achieving a preset goal as designated by one's spirituality.

Messiah (the anointed one): a Jewish and Christian term indicating one designated by God to fulfill God's will at the end time. "Christ" is the Greek word for Messiah.

Mahdi: This word is Arabic for "the guided one"—a descendant of Muhammad who will restore justice on earth. In Shi'ite Islam, a Mahdi is a messianic imam who will appear to end corruption.

Minyan: the ten adults required in Judaism to perform ritual activities such as public prayer

Mishnah: in Judaism usually used to indicate that aspect of the law that was transmitted by word of mouth.

Mitzvah / Mitzvoth: the commandments of Jewish law (613)

Moksha: Hinduism's term for liberation from the cycle of life-death-life (samsara)

Monism: the belief that everything we see and experience is actually one (the opposite of dualism). See *Monistic Spirituality* in *Glossary of Key Terms for Discussing Spiritualities.*

Monks: those who have separated themselves from everyday life and dedicated themselves to a religious ideal. Most monks live in a community of monks.

Monotheism: the belief in one eternal, creating, all-powerful God. See *Monotheistic Spirituality* below in the *Glossary of Key Terms for Discussing Spiritualities.*

Moksha: freedom from samsara –the cycle of life-death-life; the final act of breaking through to enlightenment.

Mosque: a place of public prayer for Muslims

Muslim fundamentalism: In imitation of Secular Fundamentalism and founded upon the perspective of the Traditionalists, they seek to provide new interpretations of the Quran based on additional written materials and the unique insights of charismatic individuals. Their main thrust is to provide a uniform way of life devoid of non-Islamic cultural influences.

Mysticism: In current spiritual parlance, this is a nebulous term indicating some intuitive connection with the root causes of the universe. Before the twentieth century, it usually indicated a method for uniting with God and/ or bringing about personal enlightenment.

New Thought: This is the core presupposition of many self-help movements, which is that the human mind has the inherent power to change its physical and moral environment.

Nirvana (Buddhism): the destruction of lust, hatred, and delusion and with it any sense of a permanent ego. Total freedom from all conditioning, including death, leaves us with an admission of a new existence without the images to think or desire it.

Om (Aum): a primitive chant derived from ancient Hindu rituals that, when sounded by the righteous in the proper manner, is believed to align both earth and heaven

Orthodox Christians: This term is usually used in reference to Eastern Orthodox Christians who originally looked to Constantinople, now Istanbul, for their center. The date most commonly given for the split between Eastern (Orthodox) and Western (Catholic Christianity) is 1054 CE.

Orthodox Judaism: Jews who meticulously follow all the Jewish laws and their interpretations

Pali canon: the normative list of writings for the Theravada Buddhists

Pantheism: the belief that everything and everyone is God

Paradox: anything that on the one hand is filled with contradiction and, on the other, provides us with a sense of truth and wholeness. See: *Seven Spiritual Paradoxes* below.

Pentecostal Christianity: a Christian movement that emphasizes the charismatic gifts, particularly talking in tongues and baptism in the Holy Spirit. It is the fastest growing form of Christianity.

Pharisees: an ancient Jewish movement that was the basis for rabbinic Judaism that formed in opposition to the Sadducees. They believed in resurrection and deemphasizing ritual and emphasizing the mitzvoth and prophecy.

Polytheism: the belief that many gods exist and interact with our universe

Prajna: the virtue of wisdom and insight as indicated in Buddhism's eight-fold path

Predestination: God's determination of a person's or society's life

Prophet: one who speaks for God

Protestant Christianity: a Christian movement first begun as a rejection of Medieval Roman Catholicism and an advocacy of the Bible as the sole norm of faith and faith as the sole means of recognizing God's love for us

Puja: ways of expressing one's devotion to any of the Hindu gods, such as prayerfully touching it before leaving the house

Pure Land Buddhism: a variety of Mahayana Buddhism

Quran (Quran): Muslim holy book. Muslims consider it the actual word of God as heard by Mohammad and written down by those to whom he dictated it.

Rabbi: a religious functionary in Judaism whose main concern is teaching Torah. In the United States, rabbis have become acculturated and are also seen as preachers and leaders of prayer.

Ramadan: a mandatory month of fasting in Islamic life. It is the ninth month of the Islamic calendar. The fast is from food and drink during the day. Prayer during this time is also encouraged.

Reform Judaism: Jews who accept the Torah as the inspiration for living one's life and adapting the mitzvoth to contemporary living

Reincarnation: the belief that after death a person's essence may again be born on this earth, if the person has not lived his/her pre-death life properly

Resurrection: the belief that at the end of this world all humans who have lived will once again live in some new bodily form

Revelation: God's disclosure of God's will for humanity. The written accounts of this disclosure (Christian Bible, Tanakh, and Quran) are the most common forms of acceptable revelation by the respective religions and/or spiritualities.

Rites of passage: rituals associated with the major events of one's life that result in movement from one status to another such as birth, puberty, marriage, and death.

Ritual: the repetition of word and act by an individual or community

Roman Catholic: a Christian who belongs to the Church of Rome on the global level. Usually this occurs through a local Roman Catholic Church or other religious institution.

Sabbath: In Judaism, it begins at sundown on Friday and ends at sundown on Saturday. By analogy, some Christians use the term for Sunday. In both religions, it is the weekly day of rest and religious reflection.

Sacred: separate and apart from the ordinary and deserving of respect and honor

Salvation: the attaining of perfect transcendence

Samadhi: the highest level of meditation. To some this is when the meditator becomes one with her or his object of concentration; to others, it is when a person attains a state of perfect distance from all change.

Samsara: the never-ending cycle of life and death. For humans this is a cycle of continual re-incarnation.

Samurai: Japanese warriors originating in Zen Buddhism and living a life of self-sacrifice, reverence, benevolence, filial piety and care for the elderly.

Sangha: term for Buddhist monastery or community

Satanic spirituality: This belief is twofold: this worldly or otherworldly. These are two distinct groups of writings and claims. This worldly interprets "Satan" as a natural force and everything about him is so interpreted. It concentrates on the here and now of a life of total pleasure. The otherworldly interpretation sees Satan as opposite to God and everything about this spirituality is a way of life contradictory to Christianity. Its focus is upon Satan as the father of all evil and how to cooperate with him to bring evil into our world.

Secular fundamentalism: This is a modern mentality that rejects the values inherent in the scientific method and seeks power to change the present into a future based on uniform ideas, customs, and essential experiences.

Secularism / Secularization: Three meanings dominate contemporary life: first, the Christian church has little influence on the direction of the culture (society is secularized); second, church members no longer hold to some or all of the beliefs of the church (norms of the secular world such as divorce are present in the church); third, the experience of the sacred is now also found outside the churches. The sources of this sacred experience are not always found inside the churches.

Sephardim: the descendants of those Jews who lived in Spain and Portugal before the Spanish Inquisition

Seven Spiritual Paradoxes: I am an immortal who dies. I need a "we" to be a "me." To be alive I must change and remain the same. I am one and many. My spiritual life is both free and earned; gift and purchased. I must fight to be in harmony with all. I am the same and different.

Shakti (power; might): a goddess whose power enables her worshipers to gain their inmost desires

Shaman: This term refers to a person who, much like a witch, is able to heal, cast spells, control the weather, communicate with and travel among spirits.

Sharia: the laws that govern the Muslim community

Shia (Shi'te/Shite) Islam: Shia is short for Shi'atu 'Ali – followers of Ali, the husband of Fatima, Mohammad's daughter. They accept Ali and his successors and the leaders and interpreters of Islam. They accept some Hadith that Sunni do not and thus differ in what laws should govern Islam. They are a minority within Islam.

Shinto Spirituality: the diverse spiritualities inherent to the Japanese culture

Shiva: the Hindu supreme god who is destroyer, creator, preserver, and revealer

Shruti: Hindu sacred books that are considered of divine origin

Siddhartha Gautama (563-483 BCE): the founder of Buddhism and a Buddha in his own right

Smriti: This word means "that which is remembered": foundational, but secondary to Sruti, sacred texts in Hinduism.

Soul: The essence of a person that some see as immortal and incorporeal; others, as inherently linked to the body; others, as the source of thought and will.

Spirit: This term has many and sometimes contradictory meanings, among which are similarity to soul, God, ghost, and the inner meaning of the person, event, or community.

Spiritual: There are many meanings of this term, all of which are dependent on the term "spirit." In this text, it refers to the experience and/or the actuation of transcendence.

Spiritual Feelings (experiences): See the *Glossary of Key Terms for Discussing Spiritualities*—the basis of all spirituality.

Spiritual Idol: See the *Glossary of Key Terms for Discussing Spiritualities*.

Spiritual Signposts: See the *Glossary of Key Terms for Discussing Spiritualities*

Spiritual Sources: See the *Glossary of Key Terms for Discussing Spiritualities*.

Spiritual: See the *Glossary of Key Terms for Discussing Spiritualities*.

Stupa: something built, usually mound-like and circular, that has close association with Buddha, such as his relics, his memory, or a statue.

Sufi Islam/Sufism: a mystical movement within Islam that developed methods for experiencing God's presence

Sunni Islam: This group represents the majority of Muslims who follow the law as established by the Quran, the Hadith, and the consensus of the Muslim community.

Sunyata (emptiness): total change in ourselves and in our environment

Sura (sutra): a way of dividing the Quran into paragraphs or chapter. There are 114 suras in the Quran.

Survival Spirituality: See *Glossary of Key Terms for Discussing Spiritualities*

Symbol: anything and/or person that places us in contact with a reality beyond our self. It has many meanings and provides diverse experiences. For instance, an image of the American flag places us in contact with the nation it represents. To an American, this is usually a positive experience; to the Taliban, it is usually a negative experiences.

Symbol experience: the feelings associated with our coming in contact with a symbol. These may be very intense (crying, fainting, inability to talk) or slightly intense.

Symbol fact: anything and/or person without meaning and the ability to place us in contact with a reality beyond our self; for example, the actual color, cloth, and design of what we label an "American flag."

Symbolic immortality: Jay Lifton's term for the symbols that give us a sense of continuing beyond our own death.

Synagogue: the Jewish place of prayer, study, and community gatherings. The term "Shul" is used by Orthodox Jews; "temple" by Reformed Jews; "synagogue" by Conservative Jews.

Talmud: the commentary on the Torah by rabbis as contained in the Mishnah and the Gemara

Tanakh: Jewish Holy Books: Torah (law), Prophets (Nevi'im), and writings (Ketuvim)

Tantra: spiritual methods that accept the reality of the here and now while providing ways to transcend it. In the United States, this term has become associated with sexual practices that bring a deep sense of spiritual union to the partners.

Tao/Dao (China): The harmonious path which, when submitted to, fulfills us individually and socially.

Tao-te-ching (Laozi) an ancient Chinese text by Lao-Tzu written sometime before the fourth century BCE

Terminal values: those people and/or things that are ends in themselves

The Middle Way: Buddhism

Theology: the systematic and academic study of one's religion and/or spirituality

Theosophy: This movement sees the present world as an evolving consciousness that manifests itself through diverse reincarnating bodies of which the soul is one of these incarnations. The diverse religions help us evolve through these manifestations.

Thervavada Buddhism: the oldest of the forms of Buddhism. It promises total enlightenment and offers the Middle Way of Buddha as the means to achieve it.

Torah: the first five books of the Tanakh and of the Christian Old Testament. The word Torah is frequently translated as "law," but it is more a reference to God's revelation to the Jews both written and non-written.

Traditional Christians: those Christians who accept that the Christian church is the presence of Jesus in this world and accept the signposts developed over the centuries as valid and normative expressions of Jesus's way of life.

Traditionalists: those who look to a literal imitation of a former time and place to defend themselves from the perceived threat of the modern, thus transforming this present world into a better one

Traditioning: an essential process in the Co-temporalist movement, it enables the beliefs, rituals, morals, and polity of the past to change in order to provide the same empowerment to the present and the future

Transcendence: a state of total change permitted to an entity (heaven; Nirvana)

Transcendent: that which exists beyond the here and the now of everyday living. "The" transcendent is usually referred to as God.

Transcending: the process of movement and change to bring about the promise of one's spirituality (baptism; meditation).

Ummah: the community that is Islam

Upanishads (1000 BCE): a collection of texts within the Vedas that are accepted literally by Hinduism, re-interpreted by the Bhakti movement, and rejected by Jainism and Buddhism.

Vajrayana Buddhism: the Buddhism of Tibet and Tantric methods, to name a few, that promises to provide its followers with the power of enlightenment capable of being used now and in the hereafter.

Values: that which (and who) is important. They are the ideals, words, and actions we choose, prize, and act upon.

Vedanata: a synonym for one part of the Vedic texts, the Upanishads. For some it refers to those texts that enable one to come to a realization of the nature of reality itself.

Vedas (2000-800 BCE): the basic texts of Indian culture and spirituality

Vinaya: Buddhist discipline

Vishnu: the supreme Hindu god with the main task of keeping everything in existence

Wahhabi (Salafi) Islam: a reform movement within Islam advocating a strict Sharia; puritanical in nature. Saudi Arabia is a model of Wahhabism.

Wicca: a this-worldly spirituality that uses the forces of nature to bring about the desires of its adherents. Followers of Wicca usually claim to follow in the footsteps of ancient European women who worshiped ancient gods before the advent of Christianity.

Witches are viewed as two distinct lifestyles: this-worldly or otherworldly. This worldly are individuals who claim to control the forces of nature in order to bring about their wishes. Otherworldly are those who are either in the control of Satan or use Satan's power to satisfy their desires.

Wu-wei (active non-doing): The belief that if you live simply, act simply, and think simply, harmony will come.

Yahweh (YHWH): the name of God as first worshiped by the Jews and later by Christians and Muslims. Many Jews do not say this word because of its sacrality, instead replacing it with "Lord."

Yang: a force inherent to the Tao that is active, expansive, and procreative.

Yin and yang: two essential forces that constitute the Tao

Yin: a force inherent to the Tao that is passive, contracting, and negative

Yoga: In current language, yoga is both a disciplined practice of mind and body and a general designation for diverse spiritual paths to enlightenment in Hinduism.

Zakat: In Islam, this is the duty to share some of one's wealth with the poor.

Zen Buddhism (Japan): a variety of Mahayana Buddhism

Zionism: a movement within Judaism beginning in the late nineteenth century that advocated an independent homeland for all Jews. This became the state of Israel.

Zohar: a group of books that form the core of the Jewish Kabbalah

Glossary of Key Terms for Discussing Spiritualities

The basis of all spirituality is the experience of transcendence (going beyond our present existence). It offers the hope of continuance and provides the foundation for future transformations that will produce a world radically different from the present one. Other experiences sometimes constitutive to and/or flowing from the transcendent are experiences of the sacred, the mysterious, the holy, the supernatural, duty, obedience to a cause, fellow feeling, belief, discipline, dedication, and/or a power or energy beyond the individual and all humans that determines and directs where and how we live our lives.

A religious spirituality is the conscious recognition and acceptance of an institutionalized spirit of living that manifests and causes an ultimately whole, healthy, responsible, belonging, and meaningful life.

A spiritual life promises and promotes the vision and means to change the present into another, better world in the near or distant future. Both vision and means are culturally dependent. The shift in pivotal means is expressed in the spiritual true north indicated by one's spiritual compass.

Spirituality is a way of life seeking a beneficial transformation and transcendence of self and community.

Collegial spiritual listening is an ability to attend to the whole person: body, mind, and spirit. It demands we be silent and listen to silence; we hear the words the other utters as valuable; we see the actions that person make as conveyers of meaning; we honor the thoughts he expresses as sacred to him. It demands we honor her ideas as well as her feelings.

- It consists in patterns of symbols expressive of a whole.
- It is the conscious recognition and acceptance of a certain spirit or style of life as normative for present and future living.

- It promises and promotes a unique way of dealing with both mystery and paradox.
- It provides its adherents with a way of life that enables them to think and act about such real life situations as helping the poor, the suffering, others in our community, money, those of a different gender, and nature itself.
- It provides us with steady signposts for the road of life.

Spiritual listening is attending to individual and communal yearning to change the self and the world for the better as evidenced in their words and actions.

Spirituality many times is bound to the lifecycle values described by Erik Erikson that occur from childhood to old age: hope, willfulness, purposefulness, competence, fidelity, love, care, and wisdom.

Spiritualities Based on Our View of God (as distinguished from god)

Agnostic spirituality promises and promotes an ability to live wholistically in the midst of acknowledged continual uncertainty as to human betterment and positive change. Many times such agnosticism is seen as essential for living in liminal times.

Atheistic spirituality is usually defined by what it rejects—an all-powerful and knowing creator, God, of all that exists. In contemporary culture, it is many times understood by atheists to be the total adherence to the promise promoted by scientism and the means of perfection offered by the sciences.

Monistic spirituality envisions present, past, and future as one. All reality is unified in such a way that the promised use of the means provided enables the practitioners to remove the barriers that prevent them from realizing their oneness. This does not rule out the presence of gods and spirits in our present deformed state of existence. Many of these spiritualities recognize such entities as necessary beings in the human evolution to oneness. Eastern spiritualities are usually referred to as monistic.

Monotheistic spirituality envisions time as linear and history as causal of present existence. The one God who is creating this world is seen as the force that will bring it to perfection in the future. The means provided to humans sets the scene for this perfecting action. There is only one God; any other gods, spirits, and animate or inanimate realities are dependent upon God for their existence. Western spiritualities are understood to be monotheistic and may be described as dualistic.

Polytheist spirituality may exist within a cyclical, linear, or unified view of time. This world, and any possible evolutions of it, results from the interaction of gods and spirits, usually present in a non-empirical world, with this one. The power of a god or spirit is unique to each god or spirit yet it is usually envisioned within a hierarchy of gods. Eastern spiritualities are seen to be polytheistic. Western spiritualities may be also be seen as polytheistic when spirits of all sorts, such as angels and devils, are part of that spirituality, and when God is seen as also a spirit but as having supreme power over them.

Spiritualities Based on the History of Western Culture

Survival/indigenous spirituality. The promise of a perfected present in the future is promoted by the myths and rituals engaged in by individuals and community. Any imperfections of the present are overcome by using the rituals provided by tradition. In doing so the necessary food, marriage arrangements, secure personal interactions, and healthy life are enabled.

Medieval spirituality. This form of spirituality was founded on the vision and hierarchical nature of Roman Catholicism between 900 CE and 1500 CE. A life with God is promised and promoted by the proper use of sacraments and through the encouragement of habits to avoid the seven deadly sins (lust, gluttony greed, sloth, envy, anger, and pride), and to attain the virtues opposite to them (chastity, temperance, charity/generosity, diligence/hard work, patience, kindness/compassion, and humility).

Modern spirituality promises a future world made perfect through the sciences and their derivatives. Many modern spiritualities are characterized by a Secular Fundamentalist outlook with one's certitude and fellowship derived from scientific facts and theories based on the hard and soft sciences.

Liminal spiritualities are embedded with uncertainty, tentativeness, and suspicion of all ideologies and communities that demand one's total commitment over a prolonged period of time. The signposts of the past that embedded the ancient religious visions, promises, and promotions are experienced as unproductive in resolving present challenges. Yet hope is the energizing force shaping, or reshaping, these signposts. Such hope too easily attaches itself to charismatic personalities who offer a salve to present pain by energizing hope for a tomorrow obtained with little personal effort.

Spiritualities Based on Longevity and Adaptability

Classical spiritualities share the longevity and signposts of the classical religions. While the past is no predictor of the future, their ability in the past to change while remaining the same suggests they will evolve to live beyond these liminal times. Their greatest challenge, however, will be in their ability to somehow transform those aspects of their promises and promotions tied to one culture and still be recognized as the same. The current seeming necessities of environmentalism, pluralism, and gender equality are special challenges to such identity of culture and spirituality.

Classical spiritualities have existed for centuries, usually over a thousand years, and have the capacity to awaken individuals to the transcendent experiences available to them. They are composed of classic texts, music, art, ideologies, and architecture. Each spirituality has been and many times still is constitutive to the major world cultures.

- **Eastern classical spiritualities** find their origins in the religions of India (Hinduism, Buddhism, Jainism, and Sikhism) and of East Asia (Taoism, Shinto, and Confucianism).
- **Western classical spiritualities** find their origin in religions of Judaism, Christianity, and Islam.
- They share a common transcendent desire and the necessity of all five signposts. They differ significantly regarding their sense of time, deity, and humanity.

Marginal spirituality expresses the vision of those who have rejected the classical spiritualities throughout history. Their language and imagery sometimes reflect that of ancient oral cultures, and at other times the experiences and rhetoric of contemporary charismatic personalities. Most contemporary marginal spiritualities are composites of visions and signposts picked from ancient writings and imbued with contemporary language that titillates one's transcendent desires. Today the most common synonyms for marginal spiritualities are sect, cult, occult, esoteric, mystical, and metaphysical.

Spiritualities Based on an Authoritative Source of Promises and Promotions

A worldly spirituality is one that promises and promotes individual and social transformation to a clearly articulated way of life through a clearly designed process for getting there based on a current means of empirical verification, which is its authority for claims of truth.

An other worldly spirituality promises and promotes individual and social transformation to a metaphorically described way of life through processes warranted by spiritual authorities based on this-worldly reason and experience found in a book, person, ritual, religious community, or personal experience.

Spiritualities Based on Geography

American spirituality is shaped by the conviction that every spirituality should focus on the individual rather than the community, have easily understood beliefs, separate church and state, have a special book such as the Bible, an experienced spiritual leader, prayer, a personal God, a special day of worship, and a simple, clear set of laws to guide one's moral life.

Niche spirituality's vision, promises, and promotions are dependent upon one's current community and its language, culture, values, and symbols. The experience of home that is part of every spirituality is especially important here because the niche is one's physical and/or virtual home.

Spiritualities Based on a Response to Modern Culture

Traditional spirituality, different and many times at odds with its classical religious history, rejects the modern world as devoid of God's signposts and advocates a world described as "traditional." This idealized traditional world is developed within a Secular Fundamentalist milieu and enveloped with a nostalgic feeling productive of a sacral experience.

Contemporalist spirituality accepts the modern world as described by science and usually transforms this description into a prescription for spiritual life. The social sciences in particular become normative for the determination of a mature spiritual life. Although the sciences are offered as the norm, their practical application is ordinarily derived from extremely popularized versions of the results of these sciences and their relevant technologies.

Co-temporal spirituality accepts the validity of the sciences and the particular classical spirituality under consideration. Sometimes this acceptance takes the form of declaring that each sphere, the religious and the scientific, has separate norms for truth and action. One's spirituality, then, may be lived without fear of contradiction because science has nothing to do with or say to spirituality and vice versa: Science may be developed without fear of religious contradiction because it is concerned with a reality and way of life separate from it. Most of the time Co-temporal spirituality accepts truth and this world as one; it also accepts the challenge of discerning the commonality of scientific and religious truth and engages in both the scientific and religious ways of life with the conviction that both will energize and transform the world we live in.

Spiritualities Inherited from Medieval Europe (*spiritualitas*)

As a mode of being: opposite of corporality
- The *spiritual* realm (e.g. clergy)
- The *temporal* realm (e.g. laity)

As a way of acting
- *Active life* such as that involving work, family, sensuality, and the ordinary
- *Contemplative life* such as those activities comprising the mind, the ethereal, and the sacred

Five Spiritual Signposts

The five spiritual signposts are words and actions—tangible expressions of a person and/or culture that enable us to promote our spirituality and experience the promises of transcending this current life

- **Belief** many times is found in stories, songs, poetry, creeds, and formal communal declarations. It is expressive of a desire for truth and trust.

- **Ritual** is discovered in the sacred times of the day, week, month, year, and season and in the repeated prayers, expressions of joy, sorrow, and conviction of salvation. Whether as repeated expressions of belief combined with action or action alone rituals express a desire for harmony and predictability of formative actions that remind us of the past and provide hope for the future.

- **Moral or ethical norms** (doing the right thing) are the agreed-upon communal ways of acting and speaking that reflect the community's view of truthful relations to the world as they know it and expect it to become—a world of fair, loving relationships that will birth the spirituality's vision of total transformation.

- **Community** is all of us supporting one another's beliefs through ritual actions, knowing that we can depend on each other to act in a just and life giving way toward one another. The formation of a community is a reflection of a desire for togetherness, belonging, and fellow feeling.

- **Desire for transcendence** is the continually energizing force that urges us to move beyond the present to a changed future. This force, when being satisfied in a spiritual experience, is experienced as the sacred, the mysterious, the holy, the supernatural, duty, obedience to a cause, fellow feeling, belief, discipline, dedication, and/or a power or energy beyond the individual and all humans that determines and directs where and how we live our lives. The desire for, and satisfaction of transcendence, is what gives value to all the other signposts.

Spiritual Sources: Anything and everything has been found a source of spiritual life, touchstones of the sacred and transcendent. These times, places, persons, words, actions, things, and communities are believed to be a means through which one is in the presence of that power, energy, principle, or persona that sustains all existence. Spiritual Sources are the tangible constituents of each signpost.

Spiritual Idol: An idol is anything upon which we erroneously place our transcendent desires while simultaneously adopting inadequate sources and signposts to fulfill authentic ones.

FURTHER READINGS

The resources provided here are meant to aid you in your search for pertinent materials dealing with your spiritual discoveries. The books were chosen for their ability to expand on what was provided in the text. The websites were chosen to update you on materials that were in the text and to provide gateways to further discoveries.

Classical Spiritualities and Religions

- Classical Texts: Six volumes of the sacred texts of the major world religions and their embedded spiritualities: *The Tanakh* (Judaism), *The New Testament and Apocrypha* (Christianity), The *Qu'ran* (Islam), *The Analects* of Confucius (Confucianism), *The Rig Veda* (Hinduism) and *The Dhammapada* (Buddhism). *On Searching the Scriptures: Your Own or Someone Else's: A Reader's Guide to Sacred Writings and Methods of Studying* is the introductory volume by the editor, Jaroslav Pelikan: New York, Quality Paperback Book Club, 1992.
- Robert E. Van Voorst, *Anthology of World Scriptures* (Belmont, CA: Wadsworth/Cengage Learning, 2011), 11th ed. This book provides a helpful introduction to the writings of the classical religions and their associated spiritualities.

The following are two excellent series that include texts, commentaries, and reflections upon diverse spiritualities:

- Orbis press's *Traditions of Christian Spirituality Series* and *Modern Spiritual Masters Series*. For the books within each series see http://www.orbisbooks.com/msm.htm
- Paulist Press's *Classics of Western Spirituality*. The list of available books may be found at http://www.paulistpress.com/bookSearch.cgi?page=series_westernspirit

The Internet is also an invaluable tool for reading and reflecting on the classical texts. Simply type into a search engine the titles of the texts mentioned above or as found in the body of this book. The result will be a site for whatever text you are seeking. Select the translation that you are most comfortable reading. At an introductory level, the differences in translation are not that significant.

The same can be said for all the spiritualities reviewed in this text: type in their proper name and the official website will provide all the information you need for further review of their signposts. Some terms are unique to this book and will not be found on the Internet.

Marginal Spiritualities and Religions Texts

Cowan, Douglas E., and David G. Bromley. *Cults and New Religions: A Brief History* in Blackwell Brief Histories of Religion Series. New York: Wiley-Blackwell, 2007.

- Flowers, Stephen. *Lords of the Left Hand Path: A History of Spiritual Dissent*. Runa Raven Press, 1997.
- Harvey, G., and C. Hardman, eds. *Paganism Today: Wiccans, Druids, the Goddess and Ancient Earth Traditions for the Twenty-First Century*. New York: HarperCollins, 1996.
- Hutton, Ronald. *The Triumph of the Moon: A History of Modern Pagan Witchcraft*. New York: Oxford University Press, 1999.
- Ziolkowski, Theodore. *Modes of Faith: Secular Surrogates for Lost Religious Belief*. Chicago: University of Chicago Press, 2009.

Two websites may be helpful in your investigations: For a translation of some of the books of the marginal spiritualities, see the Alchemy website: http://www.levity.com/alchemy/corpherm.html.

For a collection of other commentators on the texts and developers of the tradition, see *The Hermetic Library* at http://hermetic.com/.

Classical and Marginal Spiritualities and Religions

Some comprehensive texts that provide further depth to what we have offered in this book.

- Bellah, Robert N. *Religion in Human Evolution: From the Paleolithic to the Axial Age.* Cambridge, Mass: Harvard U. Press, 2011.
- Chidester, David. *Patterns of Transcendence.* Belmont, CA: Wadsworth, 2002.
- Hemeyer, Julia Corbett. *Religion in America.* Upper Saddle River, NJ: Prentice Hall, 2006.
- Corrigan, J., Denny, F., Eire, C., and M. Jafee. *Jews, Christians, Muslims: A Comparative Introduction to Monotheistic Religions.* Upper Saddle River, NJ: Prentice Hall, 1998.
- Lindner, Eileen W. *Yearbook of American and Canadian Churches 2008.* Nashville, TN: Abington Press, 2008. This book provides essential information about religious organizations. Online access provides constantly updated information.
- Mead, Frank, and Samuel Hill. *Handbook of Denominations in the United States*, 12th ed. Nashville, TN: Abingdon, 2005. This book provides descriptions of the beliefs, worship practices, ethical imperatives, and organizational forms of the various religions in the United States.
- Laboa, Juan Maria, ed., *The Historical Atlas of Eastern and Western Christian Monasticism.* Collegeville, MN: Liturgical Press, 2003. This book provides a good overview of the development of monasticism.
- Young, William A. *The World's Religions: Worldviews and Contemporary Issues.* Englewood Cliffs, NJ: Prentice Hall, 2005.

The following web addresses provide quick access to up-to-date information concerning all the spiritualities we have reviewed in the text.

- *http:// www.religious tolerance.org/ Ontario Consultants on Religious Tolerance.*
- *http://csrs.nd.edu/* A site for the social studies study of religion.
- http://pewforum.org/about/ and http://relegions.pewforum. org/reports. This site provides basic information about specific religions, recent surveys, and opinion polls.
- http://web.archive.org/web/20060907005952/http://etext.lib. virginia.edu/relmove/ This site provides detailed profiles of more than two hundred marginal religious groups and movements.
- *http://www.about.com/religion/*
- *http://www.adherents.com/* The religions of the world are enumerated here, and descriptions of various religions are provided. Some referral sites are not as objective as first indicated.
- *http://www.beliefnet.com/* This site is devotional in orientation yet provides quick comparisons on subject matter across diverse religions, such as discussions about the end of the world.
- *http://www.thearda.com/index.asp*
- *The Association of Religion Data Archives* (ARDA) supports this site. Data included in the ARDA are submitted by the foremost religion scholars and research centers in the world. Religious membership by zip code is found here. Research ability may be limited by one's professional competence.

NOTES

[1] (NY: Penguin, 2006)

[2] (NY: Hay House, 2010)

[3] (Chicago, IL: Northfield Publishing, 2010)

[4] (Novato, CA: New World Library, 2004)

[5] (NY: Harper Collins, 2010)

[6] Stage theories are good for clearly providing what usually happens to most people. They are weak as to the final stage or stages, because these seldom happen to most people. The researchers, then, are usually imposing their own values on the data to suggest their ideal of the processes' goal.

[7] I am not equating consciousness with perception. Our consciousness is a multilayered reality. See Eric Schwitagebel, *Perplexities of Consciousness* (New York: MIT Press, 2011). A major limit to our current consciousness is our niche. See Eli Pariser, *The Filter Bubble: What the Internet Is Hiding from You* (New York: Penguin, 2011).

[8] Of course, there may be more dimensions than four, as argued in mathematics and physics. See Robin Le Poidevin, *Travels in Four Dimensions: The Enigmas of Space and Time* (New York: Oxford, 2003). A much older (1884) book, but one that is continually published because it is easy to read and understand, is Edwin Abbott's *Flatland: A Romance of Many Dimensions* (New York: Paw Prints, 2010). Most, if not all, spiritualities developed within the era of four dimensions. If there are more than four, they would be included in the "world" category. See also Bernard Carr, ed., *Universe or Multiverse?* (New York: Cambridge University Press, 2007).

[9] I realize that spiritual authorities claim to have otherworldly guarantees regarding their promises and their promotion of transformation and transcendence, but these are all based on experience in this world. It is impossible to be totally in the other world and this at the same time.

These revelations are always in this world's languages based on experiences in this world—a paradox, perhaps worthy of inclusion in the list in the next section.

[10] This absurdity is many times evidenced by the psychosocial ego defense reaction of denial among many experiencing death.

[11] See http://www.psychotherapy.com.au/TheDoubleBindTheory.pdf.

[12] Ernest Becker, *The Denial of Death* (New York: Free Press, 1973).

[13] For a summary of these views, see Joel J. Kupperman, *Theories of Human Nature* (New York: Hackett Publishing, 2011).

[14] See W. W. Meissner, "The Ignatian Paradox," in *The Way* 42, 3 (July 2003): 33-46.

[15] Although a half-century old, the following is the best review of what follows: Paul Tillich, *Dynamics of Faith* (New York: Harper & Row, 1957).

[16] This information is from 2005 as found in the Association of Religion Data Archives at http://www.thearda.com/Archive/browse.asp.

[17] An excellent historical timeline with the events of all three of these religions listed may be found in J. Corrigan, et al., *Jews, Christians, Muslims: A Comparative Introduction to Monotheistic Religions* (Upper Saddle River, N.J.: Prentice Hall, 1998), pp. 514-24.

[18] Firm dates are lost in the record keeping of the diverse religions. What I give here are from D. L. Carmody and J. T. Carmody, *Ways to the Center* (Belmont, Calif.: Wadsworth, 1989), and B. Grun, *The Timetables of History* (New York: Simon and Schuster, 1991). The timeline offered by W. A. Young, in *The World's Religions* (Englewood Cliffs, N.J.: Prentice Hall, 1995) was used for Shinto. All dates presented here were the same among these three texts.

[19] The numbers were rounded up. Percentages are exact. These are statistics from 2005. Remember that although such numbers may be very low, they have had a profound influence on their cultures of origin. See the

Association of Religion Data Archives at
http://www.thearda.com/Archive/browse.asp.

[20] Joseph Campbell, *The Power of Myth* (New York: Doubleday, 1988), pp. 22-23.

[21] This description is dependent upon Robert Bellah who coined the term "American Civil Religion" to summarize this total dedication. He does not make nationalism and Civil Religion identical. It may be found at http://www.robertbellah.com/articles_5.htm

[22] http://www.uua.org/visitors/6798.shtml.

[23] Robert D. Putnam and David E. Campbell, *American Grace: How Religion Divides and Unites* Us (New York: Simon and Schuster, 2010).

[24] For the material on life cycle change, see Erik Erikson and Joan Erikson, *The Life Cycle Completed* (New York: Norton, 1998).

THE AUTHOR

Nathan R. Kollar is professor emeritus of Religious Studies at St. John Fisher College, Rochester, NY, retired adjunct professor in the Graduate School of Education, University of Rochester, NY, and cofounder and Chair of the Board of the Center for Interfaith Studies and Dialogue at Nazareth College, Rochester, NY. He is author of *Death and Other Living Things*, *Songs of Suffering*, *Defending Religious Diversity in Public Schools* and *Spiritualities: Past, Present, and Future – An Introduction*. He is editor, among others, of *Rituals of Life and Death* and *Options in Roman Catholicism*. He has also authored over two hundred book chapters, articles, and reviews. Among his numerous awards and grants is the Trustees' Award for Distinguished Scholarly Achievement at St. John Fisher College, the highest award for a faculty member.

What reviewers are saying about *Soul Searching*.

Dr. Kollar's scholarly analysis of contemporary spiritualities and his unique wholistic approach to spirituality distinguishes this book from others. Soul Searching contains important information about spirituality for World Religions teachers and necessary things to keep in mind for interfaith leaders charged with guiding those on an interfaith spiritual journey.

Muhammad Shafiq, PhD
IIIT Chair in Interfaith Studies
Executive Director
The Hickey Center for Interfaith Studies and Dialogue
    Nazareth College, Rochester, NY

We live in a time when many individuals are searching for a spirituality that brings meaning to their busy lives. Dr. Kollar's handbook is designed to facilitate a process in which such a seeker can learn about world spiritualities and then identify a spiritual style that fulfills her or his unique individual needs. Soul Searching should be part of every professional's library for sharing with others or personal use.

Jean Landes, M.S., M.S.
Licensed Mental Health Counselor

What the reviewers have to say about *Spiritualities: Past, Present, and Future —An Introduction*

Professor Kollar has set an ambitious goal with "Spiritualities" and delivers the goods. Anyone interested in his or her own spirituality or in the spiritualities of other cultures, past and present, will find this carefully researched and highly readable volume to be a stimulating companion.

As a recognized scholar, he provides both depth and breadth in his treatment of the major traditions of spirituality which provide new insights even to those well versed in theology and the history of spirituality. He brings into the conversation many of the contemporary spiritualities which are often overlooked or devalued by mainstream theologians and shows how they are related to the classical traditions and the ways in which they respond to the demands of our age. This history is particularly important in what he calls our "liminal age." We are on the threshold of a future that is unknown and perhaps unknowable. Never has spirituality been more important but never have the traditional ones been so wanting in their responses.

Professor Kollar is not satisfied with providing intellectual and historical insights into these traditions. He is committed to provided help and guideposts to each of his readers and he or she struggles to find paths of meaning and significance. He provides highly practical methodologies that anyone can use to discover an apt spirituality or to deepen one already embrace.

It is rare to find both scholarly discipline and pastoral concern in a single work but "Spiritualities" is one of those. It deserves to be in everyone's library.

William L. Pickett, Ph.D.
Former President, St. John Fisher College
Retired Director of Pastoral Planning, Roman Catholic Diocese,
Rochester, NY

Dr. Kollar's book presents the world of spirituality in a clear, concise, easy-to-understand over view. His view of spirituality is perfect for the novice or the person who is well-schooled in the study of spirituality. The reader is led through the history of the world's great spiritualities as well as his own relationship to those spiritual awakenings. The novice finds as easy-to-understand summary of traditional spiritualities as well as a path to personal spiritual development. The well-versed finds a deeper understanding of the world of spirituality as well as a deeper understanding of himself. Both the novice and the learned can profit greatly from Dr. Kollar's book.

Lola Carol Thomas, MA
Chairperson of the English department
Teacher of Advanced Placement English
Chatfield High School
Littleton, CO

INDEX

18453896R00121

Made in the USA
Charleston, SC
04 April 2013